The
Cut Flower
Patch

Grow your own cut flowers
all year round

The
Cut Flower
Patch

Grow your own cut flowers
all year round

Louise Curley

photography by Jason Ingram

F

FRANCES LINCOLN LIMITED

PUBLISHERS

The Old Brewery, 6 Blundell Street
London, N7 9BH
United Kingdom
www.QuartoKnows.com

The Cut Flower Patch
Copyright © Frances Lincoln
   Limited 2014
Text copyright © Louise
   Curley 2014
Photographs copyright ©
   Jason Ingram 2014, except
   those listed on page 224
Garden plans copyright ©
   Louise Curley 2014

First Frances Lincoln edition
   2014

A catalogue record for this
book is available from the
British Library

ISBN 978-0-7112-3475-8

Printed in China

9 8 7

Contents

Introduction

My cut flower patch is a special place. I am writing this on a bleak, midwinter's day, and the plot may not look very remarkable at the moment. However in a few months' time the bare patch of ground will slowly start to transform into a veritable feast of flowers – a colourful patchwork that thrills me every time I see it. This is not an area that was designed to be a garden. Instead I created a space to grow flowers, which I could then cut and bring into my home.

I have always loved having flowers in the house, but five years ago I stopped buying them. The flowers on offer were appealing to me less and less; the style of the bouquets and the choice of blooms were just not what I was looking for. There was also a more pressing reason for no longer adding a bunch of flowers to my shopping trolley. We had just bought our first house and, with decorating to do and a garden to redesign, there were other priorities for our money. It was disappointing though to have our own home at last and not be able to fill it with flowers. Around the same time I came across an article about the damage the international trade in cut flowers was doing to the environment, and the poor working conditions the growers experienced. I was also becoming increasingly interested in growing our own fruit and vegetables and using our local farmers' market to do our shopping. All of these factors came together, and it seemed that the logical next step was to grow my own flowers.

At first I did this in raised beds in my back garden and then, when I took on an allotment, I decided to devote two beds on the plot to cut flowers. I was surprised at how little space I needed to produce flowers to have throughout the house from early spring to mid-autumn.

Scented daffodils are the perfect alternative to the ubiquitous red rose for Valentine's Day. Grow them on your cutting patch or buy them from specialist local growers.

Initially I made quite a few mistakes, but each year I learned which plants gave me the most flowers, which were easiest to grow and which lasted the longest once cut. I discovered that, just like digging up my own potatoes or podding my own peas, the satisfaction from growing, cutting and arranging my own flowers was huge. Every week through the spring, summer and into autumn I now pick and fill several buckets with flowers. I would never have been able to afford this number of flowers if I were to buy them.

Growing cut flowers became so addictive that I started to look at what plants would produce attractive seed heads, which I could use in autumn and winter once the flowers were no longer appearing. It was not just the happiness that growing the flowers brought me – I felt good because I knew I was doing something beneficial to the environment.

Every year billions of pounds are spent on cut flowers. Flowers make us feel better. They are the first thing we think of buying for special events or to cheer someone up; they brighten up a room and maybe even fill it with scent. But something has happened to the flowers we buy. Just like so much in our modern lives they have become part of big business. Large flower farms in South America and Africa grow plants

on vast scales to supply the ever-increasing demand for cheap blooms across the globe all year. Exotic flowers may grace our living rooms whenever we want them.

While it might seem that we now have a wide choice of flowers, the cut flower trade in fact suffers from the same problems that affect the food industry. Just as fruit and vegetables are grown for their shelf life and ability to survive the distribution chain, so too are flowers. Fruit and vegetables have been bred for yield and uniformity, and this desire for perfection has also crept into the cut flower industry.

Because we can buy carnations (*Dianthus*) and lilies year-round, we have lost the seasonality that was once so much a part of flower growing and buying. Never is this seen more than on St Valentine's Day, when millions and millions of dark red roses are sold. They have become a commodity just like everything else, and yet,

It will not just be you who will love your cut flower patch. The flowers will be an excellent source of pollen and nectar for a whole range of insects.

while many of us have realised that buying local and seasonal food is not only good for us but also the planet, it seems that the origins of the flowers we buy is less important.

Environmental dilemma

It is estimated that more than 80 per cent of blooms available to buy in the United Kingdom are imported, and because of their perishable nature many are air-freighted from the Middle East, Africa and Central and South America. An average-sized bouquet that you might pick up in a supermarket could have travelled 20,000–25,000 kilometres by the time it reaches your home.

However there is not just this obvious global impact on the environment. Flower farms in countries such as Kenya and Columbia are enormous, covering vast tracts of land. Growing on this scale makes it possible to produce cheap flowers, but any sort of intensive agriculture has its problems. Vast quantities of water are required to nurture the flowers, and this is putting pressure on a precious resource.

In recent years a number of charities and other organisations have become increasingly worried about the impact of the cut flower trade on the immediate environment around the farms and on the workers growing the flowers for us. Often the flower farms specialise in one type of flower, such as roses or carnations, but this type of monoculture allows pests and diseases to build up. To counter this problem chemicals are used – often those that are banned in Europe, such as dichlorodiphenyltrichloroethane (DDT). In countries where health and safety legislation and corporate responsibility are not so strict, workers are exposed to a potent mix of toxic chemicals.

Larkspurs make great cut flowers and, after picking, there will be plenty left for bees to enjoy.

So often the words 'sustainability', 'eco' and 'green' can turn people off. Many of us are reluctant to give up things we have grown accustomed to and enjoy, even for the sake of the planet. The great thing about growing your own cut flowers is that it is a win–win situation. You will love it and you can feel good, knowing that your flowers have not clocked up substantial transport distances, have not contributed to water shortages or habitat destruction and have not been grown using a cocktail of toxic chemicals. And, at a time when

our pollinating insects are struggling to find sources of nectar and pollen, your flowers will provide a vital place for them to feed. Seeing the flowers teeming with all manner of insects is not only satisfying but also practical. I seem to have fewer problems with pests on my fruit and vegetables, and I am sure that this is a result of encouraging beneficial insects such as ladybirds and hoverflies on to my allotment, because they in turn control pests.

Devoting some space to your own cut flowers is not just about having an abundance of flowers to pick. Creating your own cutting patch will open up a whole new world of flowers you can use for arranging, blooms with incredible scents and delicate ones that would not transport well. Your flowers will be special to you and not like any bought from the supermarket or florist. It is a great opportunity to express your individuality and tailor your arrangements to suit your home, a particular event or even as a gift for someone.

It is not a new phenomenon to be beguiled by flowers – they have been cultivated since medieval times. Although initially they were grown for their medicinal properties in monastic gardens or in those of large manor houses, the flowers were also used to decorate churches and the 'big house' for important events.

It was during the sixteenth century that growing flowers became increasingly popular,

and this included cultivating them for cutting. Scented flowers were grown, in particular, for their ability to mask the less appealing smells of the time, when streets were open sewers and bathing was an infrequent occurrence.

The first gardening books were written then, and these describe flowers being grown for their beauty and to decorate houses. Thomas Tusser's *Five Hundred Points of Good Husbandry* published in 1573, John Gerard's *Herball* of 1597 and William Lawson's *The Country Housewife's Garden* of 1617 all give fascinating insights into the flowers that were found in the cut flower patches of the day. For me it adds an extra dimension to my cut flower patch to know that many of the flowers I grow there are the same flowers that were giving pleasure and enjoyment nearly five hundred years ago.

The idea of devoting a special area to growing cut flowers is not new either. Grand houses with large gardens would have had cutting gardens, or 'reserve gardens' as they were called, which were often a part of the kitchen garden. These kitchen gardens were highly productive places, the pinnacles of self-sufficiency, providing the house with vast quantities of fruit and vegetables, and flowers were an integral part of the growing regime.

Flower growing was not just the preserve of the rich though. They would have been included in traditional cottage gardens too. There was also a greater affinity with the countryside and using plants from the hedgerows as decorations. What we now call foraging was a normal, everyday part of life. We might have lost this connection with seasonality during the twentieth century, but there are signs that attitudes are now changing. Perhaps the most high-profile example of this in recent years was the wedding of the Duke and Duchess of Cambridge in 2011, where only locally grown flowers were used and seasonality was an important factor behind their choice of blooms.

The Cut Flower Patch will show you that there are alternatives to the generic imported flowers that are so readily available, and these other solutions are kinder to the environment. This practical guide will describe how to create your own cut flower patch, from choosing the location and understanding your growing space to seed sowing and looking after your blooms. Annuals and biennials will provide the majority of your flowers, but I have also included a section on seasonal pickings from your garden, along with a spot of foraging from the hedgerows. If you grow a few plants with attractive seed heads that can be dried, it is possible to have a few vases filled with home-grown decoration even when your cut flower patch is asleep over the winter.

Early spring is the best time to start growing your cut flowers but, if inspiration strikes at another point in the year, don't worry, because there are still plans and projects you can be getting on with. Whether it is sowing biennials in summer or hardy annuals in autumn or tulip planting in late autumn, there will always be something to set you on course to creating your own cut flower patch.

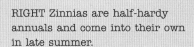

RIGHT Zinnias are half-hardy annuals and come into their own in late summer.

FAR RIGHT *Dianthus barbatus* 'Green Trick' will produce its zingy green, pom-pom flower heads right up until the first frosts.

BELOW Long-lasting, hardy scabious are the perfect cut flower.

Choosing
the right plant

Curled up in front of a roaring fire with a cup of tea, some homemade cake and a pile of seed catalogues is my favourite way of whiling away long, dark, winter nights. I love poring over the sumptuous photos, making lists and drawing up planting plans. It can be quite daunting to be faced with so many choices, especially if you do not have much space. How do you know from all those flower seeds which ones will work as cut flowers? Helpfully, many seed catalogues now include a scissors symbol to indicate varieties that are great for cutting.

My initial lists are always several times longer than the orders I actually make.

Ornamental onions (*Allium*, left) and cosmos (above) will attract bees and hoverflies to your cutting patch.

Restraint and willpower are necessary at times like this if I am not to get carried away.

Considering wildlife

When deciding what to grow in your cut flower patch it is worth bearing in mind the needs of wildlife. The countryside and ever-expanding urban areas are just not flowery enough for wildlife. Once fields and hedgerows used to be abundant with wild flowers, but the drive for increased agricultural efficiency and productivity saw an end to this. Ironically, much of the food we eat requires insect pollination. Flowers really are an essential part of our food production system, or at least they should be.

Gardeners can fill this gap to some extent but often wildlife cannot benefit from the types of flowers we grow. Over the years plant breeders have produced increasingly more fancy and elaborate flowers. Unfortunately extra petals and blowsier flowers may be attractive characteristics for some growers, but it turns out they are not for insects. Frequently the more complex the flower the harder it is for bees and other pollinators to access the pollen and nectar. The plant breeding process can also result in flowers that produce less pollen and nectar; some do not produce any.

Simple flowers with easy access to pollen and nectar are the ones to grow if you want to attract insects and provide an invaluable source of food for these beneficial creatures. The best are often single, daisy-like flowers with a ring of petals and an open centre, like cosmos and zinnias. Otherwise they might be blooms such as snapdragons, which have evolved their flower shape to fit that of a pollinating bee. Simple flowers also have a charm that is often lacking in highly bred blooms.

Although a cutting patch may be designed with the idea of picking the flowers, there are always plenty of blooms left for visiting insects to enjoy, so think about bees, butterflies and hoverflies when choosing which varieties to grow. Look for a symbol of a bee when buying seeds or plants, as this will indicate they are great for wildlife.

Protect children and pets

A surprising number of common plants such as lilies and daffodils can be poisonous. If you have children and pets around your home and garden it is wise to take a few precautions.

- Teach young children and pets not to eat garden plants and those brought indoors without prior approval.
- Store bulbs and seeds in a safe place.
- Do not leave discarded stems and flowers lying around.
- Display vases somewhere out of reach of young children and pets.
- As plants fade, watch for pollen, petals and seeds falling to the ground, where they could be picked up and eaten.
- Keep non-edible plant material away from areas of food preparation and consumption.
- To check which plants are potentially harmful to humans, take a look at the RHS website and those of charities which look after animals such as the Dogs Trust (see page 217).

Planning
a cutting patch

What makes a great cut flower?

Vase life

You might be wondering why, if there are lots of flowers in your garden, you cannot just pick them. Well, you could – but not all flowers have the right qualities to be a cut flower. It seems a shame to pick a flower that may last for weeks on the plant but, once cut, wilts and sheds its petals within minutes of cutting. Some flowers however can have a vase life of up to two weeks.

In a small space in particular it makes sense to grow flowers that will last a while once picked. For me, a flower should last at least five days before it starts to flag. All the flowers that I have included in this book will continue to look good for at least that long. The exceptions are sweet peas (*Lathyrus odoratus*) and dahlias. Sweet peas are disappointingly short-lived, surviving only three days in a vase, but their saving grace – apart from their incredible perfume – is their profligacy. For three months, they will send out flower after flower, as long as you keep gathering them and they do not go to seed. This abundance means that once your cut flowers have gone over, there will be more than enough to pick again.

Dahlia flowers can last anything from a day to a week, depending on the particular variety, so selecting the right one is important (see page 91). Despite their short vase life, dahlias are worth devoting some space to, because of the stunning array of colours and forms available. They also provide masses of cut flowers from late summer into autumn, a time of year when other plants on your cutting patch will be winding down flower production.

Some flowers just sneak into the cut flower patch. Cornflowers (*Centaurea cyanus*), for example, need to be gathered before the flowers fully open but when some colour on the buds is showing. Should you pick them in full bloom, you will be lucky to get three days out of them before they fade and turn white. Love-in-a-mist (*Nigella damascena*) can just about manage five days in a vase. If I could be more ruthless I would possibly not grow them, but they are such beautiful and unusual flowers. Also, since they have a dual purpose – producing seed pods that can be used both fresh and dried – I always manage to find a small patch for them.

The intricate flower heads of love-in-a-mist might have an exotic look about them, but they are easy to grow if you sow them direct into the ground.

Some flowers can have a vase life of up to two weeks.

Yield

In order to fill your home with blooms throughout spring and summer you need plants that are prolific flowerers. You are probably familiar with the term 'cut-and-come-again' in terms of salad crops, where you can keep cutting over the salad and it will continue to send out new leaves, but the concept is equally as relevant with cut flowers.

Hardy and half-hardy annuals will be the mainstays of your patch. They are great performers due to their biology. Their purpose is to complete their life cycles in a year by germinating, growing, flowering and setting seed in less than twelve months. They have evolved to produce as many flowers, and ultimately seeds, as possible to maximise the chances of the plant's future survival, in the form of its offspring. For a gardener, this is incredibly fortunate; if you keep on cutting the flowers and deadheading any dying blooms the plant will keep on sending out new flowers, until it eventually produces some seed, it exhausts itself or succumbs to cold weather. The best annuals will produce up to – and if you are lucky more than – three months' worth of flowers and all for the cost of a few packets of seeds.

Opportunity

In the world of the international cut flower trade, there are other considerations in deciding what makes a great cut flower. Growing and supplying on such a large scale requires uniformity in the crop, where long, straight stems and regularity in flower sizes are all-important. When it comes to growing your own, these ideas of perfection do not matter so much. In fact this is one of the reasons why having your own cutting patch is so exciting, since a whole range of flowers, otherwise unavailable from a florist or supermarket, can be grown on your cut flower patch. There are smaller blooms that make great cut flowers but, because of their size, they are rarely found commercially; fortunately there is nothing stopping you growing them. Then you simply find a few little jugs and vases, since these will be perfect for displaying snowdrops (*Galanthus*), primroses (*Primula vulgaris*) or fabulously scented stocks (*Matthiola*).

The commercial flower trade finds it difficult to grow particularly delicate flowers because they may be easily damaged in transit or just would not survive the supply chain. Because your flowers will not travel far from your patch to your home this is much less of a problem, allowing you to grow some types of poppies (*Papaver*) and delicate grass flowers, for example, which you would not be able to buy.

Picking your flowers and having them at home almost immediately is another advantage. Your cut flowers will be super-fresh, and they will not have spent days travelling from the producer to a flower auction and then to the retailer.

Growing your own blooms gives you the opportunity to develop your own flower style. I love the wildly romantic, hedgerow look. Think Jane Austen and wandering down country lanes on a summer's day, picking flowers from the hedgerows as you go. Of course it is not a good idea to strip the countryside of wild flowers, but it is easy to create the same look with your own cutting patch.

By growing highly productive annuals and grasses such as greater quaking grass (*Briza maxima*), larkspur and scabious you can pick flowers throughout summer.

Your cutting patch

A dedicated spot

It is worth devoting a particular area of ground to growing cut flowers. I treat the flowers grown here as a crop, just like any of the vegetables and fruit I also grow. You could of course dot your cut flower plants throughout your garden borders, so that they form part of your overall planting scheme, but the advantages of having a dedicated cut flower patch, however small, are numerous. It is much easier to organise the bare soil in your beds than to slot your cut flower plants in among your existing shrubs and perennials. Also many of the annuals that I will recommend farther on in the book benefit from some support, which is easier to achieve in a special patch.

I am quite a clumsy gardener – the sort that goes into the border to plant something and in the process manages to tread on newly emerging bulbs or some delicate little beauty of a flower. Having to tiptoe through a border when I want to pick some flowers invariably causes damage to some plants.

Another reason for a separate plot is that your choice of flowers for the vase may be very different from the style of your actual garden.

There is no need to worry about how a bright pink cosmos and orange dahlias will work with the rest of the plants in your borders if they are placed in a dedicated bed. Perhaps most importantly, by growing flowers as a crop in a dedicated space you can pick away without having to worry that the garden is starting to look a little bare.

Location, location, location

One of the most essential considerations when siting your cutting patch is the amount of light your potential plot receives. Pretty much all cut flowers need a good amount of sunshine so there is no point in locating your cut flower patch in a shady spot. This really is the one consideration that you cannot ignore.

Shelter is next on the list of essentials. Strong, gusty winds can cause a lot of damage, particularly to new green growth and to plants that do not have strong stems. The other, less obvious, problem that wind causes is increased moisture loss. Plants naturally lose water through their leaves, but this process is speeded up on windy days, especially if it is also hot and sunny. In these sorts of conditions plants can wilt quickly, and young, newly planted-out plants are most vulnerable, because their roots have yet to become established. Choosing a sheltered site is best, but in reality this is not always possible.

My cut flower patch is exposed to the prevailing south-westerly winds and is windy most of the time, even in summer. Planting shelter belts, hedges and natural screening are all ways to protect a site, but on a small scale the time and expense cannot always be

A dedicated patch of ground for your cut flowers means you will not feel guilty when picking.

justified. On my own allotment, I would not be allowed to use any of these methods anyway. Therefore, having accepted that my site is not perfect, I then do my best to mitigate the effects of the wind. Watering when necessary and providing sufficient support to prevent plants from falling over and stems snapping (see pages 125–8) are enough to allow my cut flowers to thrive.

In temperate climates gardeners do not tend to suffer from extreme weather. Within such regions though there are significant differences in climate. For example, in the UK the western tip of Cornwall rarely experiences frost while in the higher altitudes of northern Britain cold can linger well into spring. Another variation is in rainfall, from the high levels found in the west to the much lower levels in southern England, which can go for long periods without rain. Thus understanding a little about your climate is crucial to knowing what you can grow and when.

Frost is probably the most important aspect of climate to think about when planning and growing your cut flower patch. It affects higher altitudes, but since cold air is heavier than warm air it will also 'move' down slopes and collect in 'frost pockets'. If you live in a valley or just a dip within a village you are likely to suffer more frost. Even in your garden or on an allotment you may find areas where frost lingers.

Your last frost in spring and the first frost in autumn govern how long or short your growing season will be. Frost is particularly damaging to young, tender foliage and will determine when you can plant out half-hardy annuals and tender plants such as dahlias. The website www.gardenaction.co.uk has a list of places across the UK, USA and Australia and the very rough first and last frost dates. These dates will vary slightly from year to year so it is always worth being prepared to give your plants some protection around the cusp of the dates.

By understanding your local climate you can choose the right plants for your cut flower patch. For example, if you live in a cool-temperate area where there is a tendency for wet summers it can be difficult to grow zinnias, and if you garden somewhere with a short growing season it might make more sense to concentrate on growing hardy annuals rather than half-hardy ones.

Your soil

Understanding your soil is fundamental to the success of growing plants. Soil science is fascinating and can get quite complicated, but for growing cut flowers it is sufficient to know only the basics.

Before you do anything, check the pH level of your soil. This will tell you how acid or alkaline it is. Your soil pH affects the nutrients available to your plants. Most cut flowers prefer a neutral soil (pH7) and can cope with slightly acid (pH6.5) or slightly alkaline conditions (pH7.5). However some such as the brassica family – which includes wallflowers (*Erysimum*) and stocks (*Matthiola*) – grow much more successfully in alkaline soils.

If you discover your soil is either more acid or alkaline than these levels do not despair or think it means you will have to give up on your dreams of your own cut flowers. It is possible to change soil pH, but time, effort and expense are required. Also the fact that it is not a permanent change, and so will need to be repeated, means it is rarely worth doing.

The best solution to problem soil is to build raised beds, filling them with compost and bought-in topsoil. This may seem like considerably more effort initially, but it will be worthwhile, and once done the beds will just need an annual top-up of compost. Your raised beds need not be very deep because the annual plants you will be growing tend to have shallow root systems, so 15–20cm/6–8in deep will be fine. If you want to grow dahlias and sunflowers (*Helianthus annuus*), both of which can have bigger root systems, a slightly deeper bed would be better.

Signs of frost damage

- Leaves can appear scorched and brittle.
- Foliage and stems turn black.
- Young plants can be turned to mush as plant cells are damaged.

Avoiding frost damage

- Do not plant cut flowers in frost pockets.
- Resist the temptation to plant out too early in the season.
- Harden off plants, gradually exposing them to outdoor temperatures.
- Mulch less-hardy plants in autumn with chipped bark or compost to protect the roots.
- Lift dahlias, dry and remove any soil and then store the tubers in a frost-free area over winter.
- Use cloches or horticultural fleece to protect plants for short periods when frost is forecast.

A healthy soil with plenty of worms in it is the key to a productive cut flower patch.

A raised bed need not cost a lot to build. Seek out wood from your local timber merchant. The beds on my cutting patch were the offcuts from a local nursery school that was being clad in oak and were purchased at a reasonable cost from my local council's woodland management centre. If you do not have such a facility, see if there is a wood recycling centre nearby. Such places are becoming more popular and will have a selection of wood for sale that would otherwise go to landfill.

Try to get locally grown hardwoods such as oak (*Quercus*) or sweet chestnut (*Castanea sativa*), which are more able to cope with a cool-temperate climate and will last longer. Avoid woods that have been treated, since these are likely to have had chemicals impregnated into them to prevent rotting. If you do want to treat your wood there are eco-friendly, non-toxic

Raised beds also work really well if your soil is very stony or lacking in organic matter or if you have drainage problems. These can be issues in the gardens of new houses where builders' rubble has ended up in the soil and heavy machinery has caused compaction. The soil in raised beds also has the advantage of warming up sooner in spring, thereby allowing for earlier seed germination. For ease of use your beds should be no more than 1.25m/4ft wide, which enables you to reach the centre of the bed without having to overstretch or needing to stand on the soil.

Understanding your soil

A clay soil will retain water and nutrients well. It will not drain easily and can be prone to waterlogging. It will be slow to warm up in spring, but is fertile and if the drainage is improved is a good soil type to have in your cut flower patch.

Sandy soil drains easily and as a result can be prone to drought and nutrients leaching from the soil, but it will warm up quickly in spring.

Silty soil tends to be somewhere in between clay and sandy soil, being more fertile than sandy soil and draining more quickly than clay, but it does have the tendency to suffer from compaction.

Creating defined cut flower beds will make life much easier. They should be sufficiently narrow that you do not need to walk on the soil, which leads to compaction.

wood preservatives available. The earthworms will thank you for not introducing harmful chemicals to the soil.

It is worth creating defined beds for your cutting patch even if your soil is in great condition and the right pH. You do not need to raise the soil level, but simply edge the beds with wooden planks or old bricks, which will give your plot some structure.

Having paths between your beds is a good idea too. Access is much easier and you can walk around your cutting patch even in wet or cold weather and not need to worry about damaging the soil structure of your flower beds. Mine were made using weed-suppressing membrane covered with chipped bark, with long planks of oak bedded into shallow trenches to keep the soil in the beds and the bark on the paths. I made my paths about 90cm/36in wide, which means I can comfortably get a wheelbarrow down them. Wooden posts at the end of each bed serve the dual purpose of providing support, for netting strung across the beds, and stopping my hosepipe from being dragged across the beds and damaging my plants.

Soil texture

Soil is made up of a mix of different particles. The proportions of these define the texture of your soil, and as the particles have different properties it is worth knowing how these will affect your soil.

The easiest way to discover what type of soil you have is to make a soil sausage. Take a handful of the soil where you plan to grow your cut flowers, mix it with a little water and mould it together in your hand to form a ball. If it does not form a solid shape, your soil has a high content of sand in it. The next stage is to roll it into a sausage shape. If your soil feels smooth

---

Keep soil healthy on your cutting patch

- ✿ Dig as little as possible.
- ✿ Mulch with compost once a year, preferably in autumn.
- ✿ Walk on soil as little as possible.
- ✿ Avoid working the soil when it is frosted or wet.
- ✿ Weedkillers and fertilisers can upset the delicate balance within the soil and can particularly affect earthworms, which are vital for a healthy growing environment. This is why I choose not to use chemicals.

– almost soapy – and holds together for a while as you roll but then breaks up, your soil has a predominance of silt particles. If it feels sticky and holds together for longer, then it is mainly clay. Armed with this knowledge you can then work out how your soil texture will affect what you will grow.

Most soils are a bit of a mix, and all will benefit from the addition of compost to improve drainage, replenish nutrients and boost the numbers of creatures in the soil, which is essential for a healthy soil. Liming can also help very heavy clay soils because it causes the small clay particles to stick together, thereby improving the overall structure and drainage. The best time to spread lime is in autumn. You should consult experts for details of the quantities to use.

If all this talk of pH, soil texture and particles has put you off gardening, do not be. The great

Basic tools

- Border fork and spade
- Rake and hoe
- Trowel
- Trug
- Twine
- Secateurs
- Gloves
- Buckets
- Hosepipe or watering can

thing about the plants you will grow as cut flowers is that they are easy to cultivate and fairly undemanding. Give them the best start and they will reward you even more.

Garden tools need not be expensive. Have a look around markets, or ask friends and family if they have any spare ones lying around.

Tools

If you are starting from scratch you cannot beat old, reconditioned tools. There is something about the feel of a wooden handle, worn smooth by years of use; it is far superior to the feeling of more modern plastic and is much warmer to touch. It also makes sense to reuse these tools rather than buying new ones. Antique shops and markets are great places to get hold of old garden tools. There are also specialist suppliers online, which will have cleaned and sharpened the tools ready for use. Ask family and friends if they have an extra spade languishing in a shed that could be put to good use. I inherited the tools I use on my cut flower patch from my late grandad-in-

Seaweed facts

Also known as marl, calcified seaweed is made up of the chalky skeletons of several types of seaweeds. The combination of lime, minerals and nutrients make seaweed a great natural fertiliser. However, removing it from the seabed is difficult to do in a way that does not damage the environment. Look for a blend of lime and dried seaweed instead, to use on your cut flower patch.

law, Eddie, a keen gardener himself. It is a nice feeling to know his tools are still being used.

Preparing your site

Fork over the bottom of raised beds and then fill them with a mix of topsoil and compost. If your cut flower patch is directly on the soil, thoroughly weed the area, fork it over and mulch with compost. If you can get hold of good-quality composted green waste from your council, that is perfect just laid on the surface. The worms will do the hard work for you, drawing the compost down into the soil.

If your soil is on the acid side, a sprinkling of a seaweed and lime mix (see box, opposite) will help any flowers in the brassica family.

ABOVE Chipped bark works brilliantly as a surface for the paths within your cut flower patch. Use it on top of weed-suppressing membrane.

LEFT Green waste compost made by local councils can be great for your soil. Apply it to the surface, and the worms will incorporate it into the soil.

Planting
plans

The following planting plans will hopefully give you the inspiration and confidence to create your own cut flower beds.

There is a plan for those with a small space or who are perhaps short on time (see opposite). This bed measures 2.5 × 1.25m/8 × 4ft and would be a great starting point if you are new to gardening and growing. I have chosen flowers that are easy to germinate from seed, and some of them can be bought as plug plants from garden centres or by mail order to make life that bit easier. A mix of hardy and half-hardy annuals and biennial plants and a tender dahlia will provide you with flowers from late spring to mid-autumn. You will have enough flowers to make posies and fill small vases.

The other plans (see pages 34–5) have been designed for 3 × 1.25m/10 × 4ft beds, although they can be adapted to any space. It is best to keep each bed width to 1.25m/4ft or less, as this allows for a comfortable reach into the centre of the bed. The length of the bed is flexible and can be adapted to fit your space.

The easy beds are filled with plants that are straightforward to grow yourself from seed, and they will cope, regardless of what the weather throws at them. The advanced beds include plants that are a little fussier about the growing conditions or the weather, and some that can be a little harder to grow from seed.

If you want to plant bulbs as well, plan these to go in spots where the half-hardy

Having compiled a list of plants to grow, it will not be long before you can pick buckets full of flowers.

annuals and dahlias will ultimately be planted, allowing the foliage of the bulbs time to die back. Edge your beds with primulas and small bulbs such as grape hyacinths (*Muscari*) to maximise flower production.

I have suggested the number of plants to put in each area, but you do not need to stick rigidly to these. They are meant as guides. When I am ready to plant out I nearly always have some plants which have not germinated as well as others, and so need to tweak my plans. Planting is not meant to be about sticking to rigid rules. If you have more of one plant than another, then use what you have. Any new planting will look a little regimented initially, but as the plants develop they will fill out, creating a patchwork of flowery colour.

Small-space bed

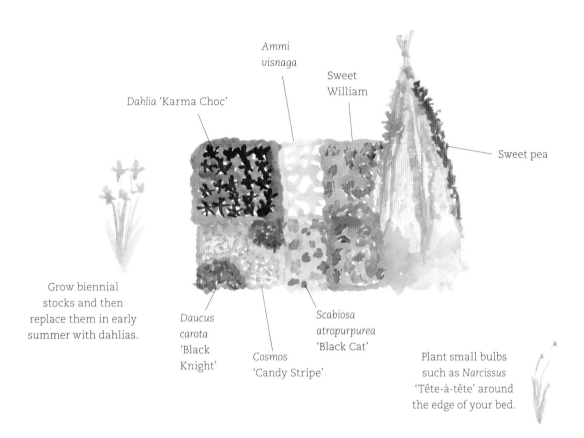

Dahlia 'Karma Choc'

Ammi
visnaga

Sweet
William

Sweet pea

Grow biennial
stocks and then
replace them in early
summer with dahlias.

Daucus
carota
'Black
Knight'

Cosmos
'Candy Stripe'

Scabiosa
atropurpurea
'Black Cat'

Plant small bulbs
such as Narcissus
'Tête-à-tête' around
the edge of your bed.

Shopping list

- ✿ 1 × Dahlia 'Karma Choc'
- ✿ 2 × Ammi visnaga
- ✿ 4 × Sweet William (Dianthus barbatus)
- ✿ 12 × Sweet pea (Lathyrus odoratus)
- ✿ 30 × Narcissus 'Tête-à-tête'
- ✿ 2 × Scabiosa atropurpurea 'Black Cat'
- ✿ 2 × Cosmos bipinnatus 'Candy Stripe'
- ✿ 2 × Daucus carota 'Black Knight'
- ✿ 6 × Biennial stocks (Matthiola)

Easy beds

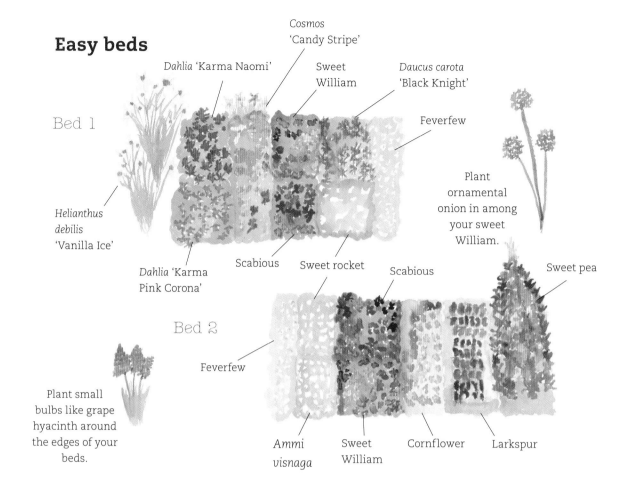

Bed 1

Cosmos 'Candy Stripe'

Dahlia 'Karma Naomi'

Sweet William

Daucus carota 'Black Knight'

Feverfew

Plant ornamental onion in among your sweet William.

Helianthus debilis 'Vanilla Ice'

Dahlia 'Karma Pink Corona'

Scabious

Sweet rocket

Scabious

Sweet pea

Bed 2

Feverfew

Ammi visnaga

Sweet William

Cornflower

Larkspur

Plant small bulbs like grape hyacinth around the edges of your beds.

Shopping list: Bed 1

- 1 × *Dahlia* 'Karma Naomi'
- 3 × *Cosmos* 'Candy Stripe'
- 2 × Sweet William (*Dianthus barbatus*)
- 2 × *Daucus carota* 'Black Knight'
- 3 × Feverfew (*Tanacetum parthenium*)
- 20 × Ornamental onion (*Allium*)
- 2 × Sweet rocket (*Hesperis matronalis*)
- 3 × Scabious
- 1 × *Dahlia* 'Karma Pink Corona'
- 2 × *Helianthus debilis* 'Vanilla Ice'

Shopping list: Bed 2

- 2 × Sweet rocket (*Hesperis matronalis*)
- 3 × Scabious
- 12 × Sweet pea (*Lathyrus odoratus*)
- 4 × Larkspur (*Consolida*)
- 5 × Cornflower (*Centaurea cyanus*)
- 2 × Sweet William (*Dianthus barbatus*)
- 2 × *Ammi visnaga*
- 30 × Grape hyacinth (*Muscari*)
- 3 × Feverfew (*Tanacetum parthenium*)

Advanced beds

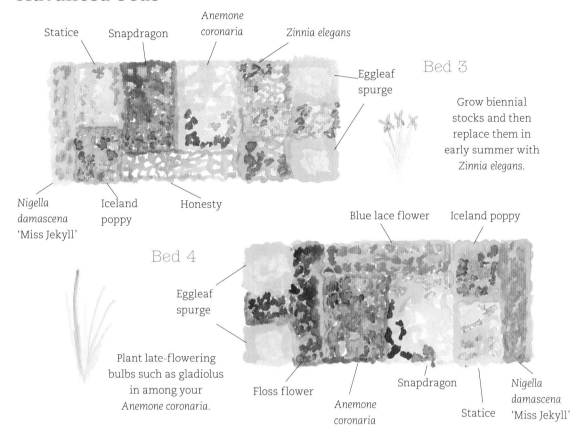

Statice

Snapdragon

Anemone coronaria

Zinnia elegans

Eggleaf spurge

Bed 3

Grow biennial stocks and then replace them in early summer with *Zinnia elegans*.

Nigella damascena 'Miss Jekyll'

Iceland poppy

Honesty

Bed 4

Eggleaf spurge

Plant late-flowering bulbs such as gladiolus in among your *Anemone coronaria*.

Blue lace flower

Iceland poppy

Floss flower

Anemone coronaria

Snapdragon

Statice

Nigella damascena 'Miss Jekyll'

Shopping list: Bed 3

- 2 × Statice (*Limonium sinuatum*)
- 3 × Snapdragon (*Antirrhinum*)
- 4 × *Anemone coronaria*
- 4 × *Zinnia elegans*
- 2 × Eggleaf spurge (*Euphorbia oblongata*)
- 4 × Biennial stocks (*Matthiola*)
- 4 × Honesty (*Lunaria annua*)
- 2 × Iceland poppy (*Papaver nudicaule*)
- 6 × *Nigella damascena* 'Miss Jekyll'
- 8 × Gladiolus

Shopping list: Bed 4

- 5 × Blue lace flower (*Trachymene coerulea*)
- 2 × Iceland poppy (*Papaver nudicaule*)
- 6 × *Nigella damascena* 'Miss Jekyll'
- 2 × Statice (*Limonium sinuatum*)
- 3 × Snapdragon (*Antirrhinum*)
- 4 × *Anemone coronaria*
- 5 × Floss flower (*Ageratum houstonianum*)
- 2 × Eggleaf spurge (*Euphorbia oblongata*)
- 8 × Gladiolus

Annuals
& biennials

Recommended
cut flowers

This section of the book will focus on the flowers that I think deserve a place on a cut flower patch. I have made my selection from my own experience of growing with limited space. There are three main types of plant that will provide the bulk of your cut flowers: hardy annuals, half-hardy annuals and biennials.

Hardy annuals can be sown either in early autumn to overwinter or between early and late spring to flower that year. By doing both, it is possible to have flowers from late spring, right through to the first frosts. Half-hardy annuals come from warmer climates and will be damaged by frosts. They can be sown in mid-spring under cover and then planted out when the risk of frost has passed, or you can sow directly in late spring when the soil has warmed up. These plants really come into their own from late summer onwards and will provide interest well into autumn. Biennials have been somewhat neglected in recent years. Fortunately they are cheap and easy to grow from seed in early and midsummer, when there is space on the windowsill and in the cold frame for a few newly sown seed trays.

The key in a small space is to have a balance of these three types of plants to maximise the amount of flowers you can pick from your cut flower patch. The following plants by no means form an exhaustive list but are plants that have performed well for me in my small space.

Sow some cornflowers in early autumn for a late spring crop the following year.

What are annuals and biennials?

Hardy annuals grow, flower and set seed in one year. They are hardy so can cope with cold temperatures and frost. Half-hardy annuals are killed by frost and, if you live in a cold-temperate climate, will need resowing each year. They also require warmth to germinate. Biennials put on growth in the first year and flower the following year.

Hardy annuals

Common name **Cornflower**

Latin name *Centaurea cyanus*

Family **Asteraceae**

Hardy annual

Why grow it? **Gives a naturalistic feel to arrangements**

Cornflower

A native of Europe, cornflowers used to be a common sight growing on arable land, creating a haze of blue, which must have been a stunning sight in early summer. Despite this beauty it was seen as a weed. With the need to increase food production and the subsequent intensification of agriculture, especially in the twentieth century, cornflowers disappeared from the countryside. In fact the wild-growing cornflower was classed as endangered at one point and is still under threat.

The striking blue colour, which gave the plant its old common name of bluebottle, has meant

Cornflowers are the perfect flowers for creating a meadow feel to an arrangement. Mix them with grasses and foraged weeds.

they have long been popular as a cut flower and were often picked by farm labourers, then bunched and sold so they could make some additional money. The cornflower is the national flower of Germany and Estonia and, in France, where it is known as *bleuet de France*, it is a symbol of Armistice Day, playing the same role as a poppy does in the UK.

Cornflowers are an easy flower to grow. Since they have a tall upright habit, wiry narrow stems and thin, lance-shaped leaves, they take up little space.

In addition to their common blue flowers, they are also available in other colours. 'Black Ball', the colour of a rich, dark red wine, looks stunning arranged with lime-greens and acid-yellows and, unlike the blue variety, does not fade to white as it ages. There are also pink and white varieties.

A hardy annual, this is one that you can sow in autumn for an early flowering the following year or you can sow between early and late spring for blooms in 10–12 weeks. Cornflowers sown the previous year tend to produce stockier and taller plants and can reach 90cm/36in in height. Spring-sown plants are more likely to be 70cm/28in tall.

When to sow Early autumn and early to late spring. Can be sown directly into the soil or into trays indoors.

Plant out From early spring.

Flowers Late spring from autumn sowing; early summer onwards from spring sowings.

Pinching out Yes, when about 15cm/6in tall.

Growing conditions Full sun. Does best on poor soils.

To feed or not to feed Not necessary.

Height 60–90cm/24–36in.

Spread 20cm/8in.

Spacing 25–30cm/10–12in.

Support Will need support. Pea netting or twine and canes.

Recommended varieties 'Blue Boy'; 'Black Ball'. For a mix of pinks, whites and blues try 'Polka Dot Mixed'. For scented and shaggy-looking flowers try *Amberboa moschata*, syn. *Centaurea moschata*.

When to pick Do this when colour starts to show on the buds. If you pick too early, the flowers may not open at all. If you harvest them once fully open, they will last only a few days.

Conditioning None needed.

Larkspur

An annual plant similar to a delphinium, larkspur is perfect for the cut flower patch. It is a smaller plant than its perennial cousin, with more delicate foliage and flowers, and is a more prolific flowerer. Its tall slender stems are covered in buds, with the flowers opening gradually from the bottom upwards. They have an excellent vase life of up to two weeks – more if you can keep them somewhere cool.

Also known as 'doubtful knight's spur' or 'rocket larkspur', the plant is native to the western Mediterranean, where it produces green clumps of attractive feathery foliage from which the tall spires appear. The flowers are flat with a spur at the back, like a columbine (*Aquilegia*), and come in a variety of colours including pink, white and dark purple.

Larkspurs are easy to grow, but are best started off indoors as they are particularly tasty to slugs and snails. Grow on a windowsill, or in a cold frame or greenhouse, until they are good-sized plants, before you plant them out. If you keep picking or deadheading, they will continue to produce flowers. I love the stems arranged

Create a cottage garden look to your posies and bouquets with the tall spires of larkspur.

Common name **Larkspur**
Latin name ***Consolida ajacis***
Family **Ranunculaceae**
Hardy annual
Why grow it? **Tall spires of flowers to add height to your arrangements**

simply in a vase on their own, but they look equally good as part of a larger arrangement, providing another layer to the flowers by adding height. Snip off any blooms as they die to keep the stalks looking tidy. You can even use the petals dried for confetti. Spread out individual petals on paper towel and put them somewhere dry, warm and out of direct sunlight – an airing cupboard is ideal. The petals take a few weeks to be completely dry, then keep in airtight containers until you want to use them. Larkspur seeds are poisonous so store them away from children and pets.

When to sow Sow in early autumn and early spring.
Plant out In mid- and late spring.
Flowers Late spring from autumn sowing; early summer from spring sowing. Will continue to flower for over two months.
Pinching out Pinch out growing tips when about 10cm/4in tall.
Growing conditions Moderately fertile soil is needed. Full sun and well-drained soil.
To feed or not to feed A mulch with compost in autumn or spring is enough.
Height 80cm/32in.
Spread 30cm/12in.
Spacing 35–40cm/14–16in.
Support Yes, either individually with canes or through pea netting.
Recommended varieties Seeds are available in mixed colours with 'Giant Imperial' offering a good range of white, pinks and purples. It is possible to get seed packets of single colours too.
When to pick When the bottommost flowers first open.
Conditioning Leave for several hours, or overnight, in cool water.

Opium poppy

I have included this variety of poppy not for its flowers but for its seed pods. It is grown in various parts of the world for the chemical compounds within the milky latex inside the plant. There can be few plants which, on one hand, do so much good by providing a vital source of painkillers, but, on the other, have also caused so much suffering as a result of the illegal drugs trade. It is hard when you look at the delicately beautiful flowers, and their papery petals fluttering in the breeze, to equate war, crime and addiction with this plant, synonymous with Afghanistan. There are now farmers in the UK who have been granted licences by the government to grow opium poppies as a crop to supply pharmaceutical companies with morphine. All parts of the plant are toxic, although once the seeds are completely ripe they are edible and are the poppy seeds you find in breads and cakes.

Opium poppy is safe enough to grow on the cut flower patch as long as you take sensible

Common name **Opium poppy**

Latin name *Papaver somniferum*

Family **Papaveraceae**

Hardy annual

Why grow it? **For their beautiful and intricate seed pods**

Grow opium poppies for their seed heads. While you wait for them to form, both you and the bees can enjoy the flowers.

precautions. As cut flowers they are not great, but leave the flowers on the plant, letting them fade and go to seed, and they produce the most amazingly beautiful seed pods. They swell into little globes, turning a glaucous blue colour, and have a flat top. As the seed head ripens the top becomes more pronounced, lifting and revealing tiny holes underneath. Like a botanical pepper pot the slightest movement of the stem shakes the pod and hundreds of tiny, blackish grey seeds fall out of the holes, scattering on to the surrounding earth. Pick the seed heads before the seeds have ripened. You can use them straightaway mixed with other flowers, or dry them, bunching the stems together and putting them head first into paper bags and hanging them somewhere warm and dry. Each bag will catch the seeds, which you can sow the following year. The seed heads will also be preserved for use as decoration in autumn and winter.

When to sow Directly into the ground in early autumn or mid-spring or in modules in spring.

Plant out From mid-spring to early summer.

Flowers From early summer to early autumn.

Pinching out Not necessary.

Growing conditions Full sun; well-drained and poor soil.

To feed or not to feed Do not feed.

Height 70cm/28in.

Spread 25cm/10in.

Spacing 25cm/10in.

Support Not necessary.

Recommended varieties Opium poppy hybridises very easily so there are lots of varieties to choose from. Even though you are growing them for the seed pods you may as well pick ones with flowers you like. There are doubles with shaggy flower heads or peony-type flowers with intricately layered petals. 'The Giant' produces good-sized seed heads, or why not try 'Hen and Chickens'? Its unusual clusters of smaller seed heads surround the main seed pod like a hen with her brood of chicks.

When handling opium poppies take precautions such as wearing gloves and washing your hands afterwards; also clean tools after use.

When to pick Pick when the seed pods have swollen but not yet opened and scattered their seeds.

Conditioning None needed.

Love-in-a-mist

The name love-in-a-mist alludes to the flowers held on stems among a haze of feathery, fennel-like foliage. This quintessential cottage garden plant, which has been grown in Britain since Elizabethan times, actually originates from the southern Mediterranean, the Balkans and North Africa. Its native countries give an indication as to the growing conditions it prefers – well-drained, light soils and full sun. Its botanical name is derived from the Latin for black, *nigellus*, referring to the colour of

the seeds. The delicate papery petals remind me of an Elizabethan ruff collar and provide the perfect background for the bright green, squiggly, sculptural anthers and stamens in the centre of the flower.

Love-in-a-mist forms tall slender plants, so you can fit quite a lot of plants into a small space. The flowering season can be short-lived and, while cutting the flowers obviously helps to prolong flowering, if any plants do go to seed this is no great problem, since the seed pods themselves are particularly attractive in arrangements. You can use the seed pods fresh or dry in arrangements. They swell and look like stripey balloons with a spiky top. I prefer to grow just one crop of love-in-a-mist, enjoy the flowers while they last, then pick and dry the seed pods. If you sow them in autumn or early spring they will have finished flowering by midsummer. If you would like love-in-a-mist throughout the summer, simply sow batches of seed every three weeks from mid-spring to midsummer, to guarantee a successional crop.

This annual hates root disturbance so it is best to sow its seeds directly into the ground. It is possible to sow into modules, and as long as they do not become root-bound they should transplant happily. If your soil is mainly clay or you live somewhere prone to heavy rainfall, it is a good idea to incorporate some grit into the soil before sowing, to improve drainage. Do not add any compost or manure to the patch, as annual flowers like love-in-a-mist thrive on poorer soils; any extra nutrients will make them produce lots of lush leafy growth and few flowers, which is no good, particularly on a cutting patch.

Love-in-a-mist is a good, dual-purpose cutting patch crop, with intricate flowers and striking seed heads.

Common name **Love-in-a-mist**
Latin name *Nigella damascena*
Family **Ranunculaceae**
Hardy annual
Why grow it? **Romantic flowers perfect**
for a wedding; also gorgeous
seed pods

When to sow Directly into the ground in early autumn and in early spring to early summer. For successional crops sow batches about a month apart.

Flowers Late spring from autumn sowing; midsummer from spring sowing.

Pinching out Not necessary.

Growing conditions Full sun; well-drained and poor soil.

To feed or not to feed Do not feed.

Height 50cm/20in.

Spread 25cm/10in.

Spacing 25cm/10in.

Support Grow through some pea netting.

Recommended varieties Blue 'Miss Jekyll'; 'Persian Rose' is a very pretty pink variety; 'Double White' for pure white flowers that would work particularly well in wedding arrangements; *N. hispanica* for its particularly fancy, dark red stamens and beautiful, deep blue petals.

When to pick When petals first start to unfurl. For seed pods when they are still green.

Conditioning None needed.

Scabious

There are annual and perennial scabious varieties, but it is the annuals that are the most prolific flowerers and best for the cutting patch. Although a member of the teasel family, it is hard to see the family resemblance when you see the flowers, but the seed heads do look a little teasel-like. *Scabiosa atropurpurea* is native to southern Europe and is also known as the Mediterranean sweet scabious. The flowers have a sweet scent, although it is not especially strong. It is thought that the name scabious derives from the Latin 'to scratch', *scabere*, and refers to the belief that the plant had properties for curing skin conditions.

In 2012, when my garden experienced seemingly endless rain and low light levels throughout summer, my scabious plants were one of the best performers on my cut flower patch. One of their greatest attributes, in my opinion, is that they can be used not just when they are in full bloom. They look so beautiful in bud that I like to pick them at this stage too,

Common name **Scabious or pincushion flower**
Latin name ***Scabiosa atropurpurea, S. stellata***
Family **Dipsacaceae**
Hardy annual
Why grow it? **Long-lasting flowers; unusual seed heads; great for insects**

with the tightly packed petals giving a hint of the colour that is to come and the ring of green bracts forming a collar around the flower bud. Some will go on to open into the full flower; others may not, but this is not a problem as they add something to an arrangement in their simple bud form. And if that was not enough, the seed heads are attractive too, and look

pretty added to arrangements. This is a great advantage of growing your own flowers, being able to cut flowers at these different stages.

Scabiosa stellata 'Ping Pong' is an annual with light blue flowers, which are beautiful, but it is the seed pods that are really striking. Globe-shaped seed heads, each divided into small pockets where the seed is held, form on the plant. The pods are papery and so unusual. You can use them straightaway mixed with fresh flowers or store them to put with other dried seed heads and grasses in the autumn and winter.

When to sow Early autumn and early spring.
Plant out Mid- and late spring.
Flowers Early summer to the autumn frosts.
Pinching out Not necessary.
Growing conditions Full sun and well-drained soil.
To feed or not to feed Well-rotted compost or mushroom compost used as mulch in autumn or dug into the soil in spring.
Height 70–90cm/28–36in.
Spread 35cm/14in.
Spacing 35–40cm/14–16in.
Support Tall, so needs support. Growing through pea netting works well.
Recommended varieties *Scabiosa atropurpurea* 'Black Cat' and 'Tall Double Mix'. *Scabiosa stellata* 'Ping Pong' for blue flowers and stunning seed heads.
When to pick At any stage. The flower buds look great, although may not open into full flowers if harvested at this stage.
Conditioning None required.

LEFT *Scabious atropurpurea*
RIGHT *Scabious stellata* 'Ping Pong'

Sunflower

The name originates from the Greek for sun, *helios*, and flower, *anthos*. This link with the sun makes it unsurprising that many of the early civilisations were inspired by the plant. For the Incas and Aztecs, sunflowers represented their sun gods, and Native American Indians would place bowls of the seeds on the burial sites of their dead. It was in central and southern America that Spanish explorers came across sunflowers for the first time and took the seeds back with them to Europe.

Sunflowers are perhaps one of the first flowers we grow as children – our introduction to the world of planting and growing. They are easy to grow and the large, bright cheerful flower heads cannot fail to make you smile. It is worth choosing the variety carefully, particularly on a small plot, as some are much more suitable for cutting than others. There are both annual and perennial types, but annuals are the ones you want on your cutting patch. Some sunflowers can grow to significant heights and have huge, dinner-plate-sized flower heads; these are great fun for children to grow but not good cut flower material. It is probably best not to need a step ladder to get to your flowers when you want to pick them. I choose varieties that grow to about 1.5m/5ft and have branching stems. This means more flowers, unlike some varieties which tend to develop one thick stem with only a few flower heads or even just a solitary flower. Sunflowers produce a lot of pollen, which is great for insects but not so useful for a cream carpet when they shed their pollen everywhere. F1 hybrids produce little or no pollen, which makes them more appealing as cut flowers, but their lack of pollen makes them much less wildlife-friendly – so it can be a hard choice to make. I prefer to grow one of the *debilis* varieties. *Helianthus debilis* 'Vanilla Ice', for example, produces masses of much smaller flowers, but they still have the classic sunflower appearance. This variety bears pale yellow flowers on strong sturdy plants with lots of branching stems and grows to about 1.5m/5ft. It does shed some pollen but because the flowers

Common name **Sunflower**
Latin name ***Helianthus annuus,***
     H. debilis
Family **Asteraceae**
Hardy annual
Why grow it? **Bright cheerful flowers**

Cheerful sunflowers are guaranteed to brighten up any room.

are smaller the quantities are not as significant. I also find the smaller flowers are much easier to use when mixed with other blooms. The larger flower heads look great gathered together in a large bunch in homage to Van Gogh's painting, but they are difficult to combine with other blooms. The weight of the stems and larger flower heads can also be surprisingly heavy, so use a sturdy vase if you do grow these types.

When to sow Indoors in early spring. Outdoors in mid-spring.

Plant out Mid- to late spring. *Helianthus debilis* varieties are prone to frost damage so give some extra protection with a cloche.

Flowers Midsummer to autumn.

Pinching out Pinch out when about 20cm/8in tall. Some varieties are naturally branching and do not need pinching out although doing so can help to reduce their eventual height and encourage sturdier plants.

Growing conditions Full sun and fertile, well-drained soil.

To feed or not to feed They will benefit from a comfrey feed while in flower.

Height 'Vanilla Ice' grows to about 1.5m/5ft.

Spread 50cm/20in. By pinching out you will create bushier plants, which need more space than one single stem.

Spacing 50cm/20in.

Support Sturdy posts pushed into the ground.

Recommended varieties *Helianthus debilis* 'Vanilla Ice'; *H. annuus* 'Valentine'.

When to pick As the petals start to unfurl.

Conditioning None needed.

The smaller-headed varieties of sunflower such as 'Vanilla Ice' work well in arrangements.

Common name **Sweet pea**
Latin name *Lathyrus odoratus*
Family **Papilionaceae**
Hardy annual
Why grow it? **Incredible scent; long
picking season**

Sweet pea

The first recorded evidence of sweet peas dates from the 1600s. These early sweet peas had small flowers but a powerful scent that particularly captivated a monk, Francesco Cupani, on the island of Sicily. He was so taken with them that he sent a package of seeds to Robert Uvedale, an English schoolmaster and horticulturalist. Dr Uvedale was one of the first people to have a hothouse in seventeenth-century Britain and had become known for growing exotics. It is now believed that sweet pea 'Cupani' is actually the wild species from which all other sweet peas derive. This variety is still available and bears the strongest of all sweet pea scents.

It is possible to buy sweet peas now as cut flowers, but the varieties most often grown by commercial growers are those with long flower stems, large flower heads and longevity once cut. Unfortunately fragrance loses out, and yet this is surely what we are mainly looking for when choosing sweet peas.

The most fragrant tend to be the older varieties, but these generally produce much shorter stems and have less blowsy flowers, which to some means they are less attractive. They also do not last very long once cut. I prefer to grow the most highly scented varieties, and while these may last only two to three days once picked it is not an issue because one of the great joys of sweet peas is that they are so productive. By the time my vase of blooms has been emptied on to the compost heap I have plenty more to pick.

Sweet peas are so easy to grow. Their seeds are like little bullets with hard seed cases. There is much debate about whether this seed casing needs to be scratched with a knife or soaked prior to sowing, to allow moisture in

The flowers of sweet peas may not last very long once picked, but I cannot imagine my cutting patch without them.

the compost to enter the seed and initiate germination. My own experience suggests neither is necessary, and I have not had any problems with seeds germinating. If you do want to soak the seeds, place them in a container in some water overnight and then sow the following day.

The other debate is when to sow sweet peas. Some swear by doing this in autumn, but I prefer to sow in late winter into tall pots – that is, pots that clematis or other climbers came in from the garden centre or nursery. Sweet peas produce long roots and perform much better when they have a substantial root system, finding it easier to cope with dry spells, and they will suffer less from mildew. I sow five seeds in a pot of multipurpose compost, pushing them in about 1cm/½in deep. Water and place the pot somewhere frost-free. A windowsill, cold frame or greenhouse is perfect. Seedlings should start to appear in 2–3 weeks.

To get a succession of flowers right through until autumn you can sow some more in mid-spring. The most important thing to remember with sweet peas is that once they are flowering you must keep picking them. If you see any flowers that have died, snip them off. To get the longest season of production do not let the flowers go to seed.

The choice of sweet peas is vast. Some seed catalogues and seed packets will rate the strength of the scent. Look out for the old-fashioned types and Grandifloras. The information will often say these do not make good cut flowers, but this is because they have shorter stems and a reduced vase life. If scent is most important to you, opt for these varieties.

When to sow Indoors in autumn and late winter/early spring. Outdoors in mid-spring.

Plant out Mid- to late spring.

Flowers Late spring (from early sowings) through into autumn.

Pinching out Yes, when the plants have four sets of true leaves.

Growing conditions Full sun and rich soil.

To feed or not to feed Sweet peas need lots of food. Add compost, manure or comfrey pellets to the planting holes. Apply liquid comfrey feed once they are flowering.

Height 1.75m/6ft.

Spread Tall climbing plants.

Spacing Plant two sweet pea plants at the base of each beanpole (see page 128).

Support Needs support, either a wigwam of canes/beanpoles or up netting.

Recommended varieties 'Fire and Ice' is my current favourite – a modern Grandiflora, it has longer stems, incredible scent and lasts longer in a vase than other varieties. 'Mrs Collier' produces delicate ivory blooms and 'Prince Edward of York' has small cerise and magenta flowers; both have great perfume.

When to pick When the first flower is just about to open.

Conditioning None needed.

I like to sow sweet peas into tall clematis pots to give their roots space to develop.

Half-hardy annuals

Floss flower

I have to admit I was never really a fan of this plant, as I had only ever seen the small varieties in module trays in garden centres destined for bedding displays or containers. I have never really understood the fascination with growing these dwarf varieties. It is like gardening for Lilliputians. I like some height in my garden, and small dumpy little stems do not make great cutting material. But then I came across some new plants bred to be taller; these were perfect for picking, and the soft fluffy flowers you do not get round to picking will be much appreciated by passing butterflies.

Common name **Floss flower**
Latin name *Ageratum houstonianum*
Family **Asteraceae**
Half-hardy annual
Why grow it? **Stunning blue flowers that you will struggle to buy**

When to sow Indoors in late winter. Give some extra warmth from a heated propagator.

Plant out After the last frost.

Flowers Early summer to early autumn.

Pinching out Yes, when plant has five true leaves, pinch out top 2.5cm/1in of stem.

Growing conditions Full sun and fertile but well-drained soil.

To feed or not to feed Comfrey fertiliser will promote more flowers; do not overfeed with nitrogen.

Height 50–65cm/20–26in.

Spread 20cm/8in.

Spacing 25–30cm/10–12in.

Support Through pea netting.

Recommended varieties 'Everest Blue'; 'Blue Horizon'; and for pink flowers 'Red Sea'.

Floss flower will bloom all summer long, producing flowers that will last more than a week in a vase.

When to pick Cut when half of the flowers on the head are open.

Conditioning Place in tepid water for several hours or overnight before arranging.

Cosmos

This native of Mexico is a superb plant for the cutting patch and, bearing in mind its place of origin, surprisingly easy to grow in a cool-temperate climate. Although happiest in warm sunshine and well-drained soil, my plants have coped astonishingly well even in very wet summers. Cosmos is probably one of the most prolific of all the cut flowers I have suggested. You will find a whole range of pinks, crimsons and also pure white; for something a bit different try *C. sulphureus* 'Bright Lights' – a mix of yellows and oranges. There is a choice of flower form too, from the simplest, daisy-like flowers of 'Purity' to 'Seashells', with its unusual petals that curve round on themselves to form tubes, or 'Double Click' with more layers of petals and raggedy edges that

Common name **Cosmos**

Latin name ***Cosmos bipinnatus***, **C. sulphureus**

Family **Asteraceae**

Half-hardy annual

Why grow it? **One of the most prolific flowerers**

look as if they have been snipped by scissors. Heights start from the short Sonata Series cosmos, which can often be found as small plants in garden centres aimed at the bedding-plant market. They tend to grow no taller than 50cm/20in, but have large flower heads. They will flower earlier than taller varieties and are a good choice if you live somewhere very exposed and windy. The flowers of Sonata Series cosmos however do not have the same delicacy as other varieties and in my experience are not so prolific as some of the taller types. 'Purity' for example can grow up to 1.5m/5ft and will definitely need support. It has such an ethereal quality, and the exquisite white flowers look beautiful arranged on their own or with other flowers. Apart from slugs and snails being partial to the young plants they grow healthily and are trouble-free throughout the season. For any varieties that grow more than 60cm/24in tall, staking or support of some form is essential (see pages 125–6). Cosmos might look like sturdy plants, but the stems will snap in a heavy rainstorm in summer or on a windy day in early autumn.

When to sow Indoors in mid-spring. Outdoors in late spring.

Plant out After last frost.

Flowers Midsummer until the first autumn frost.

Pinching out When the plant is about 15cm/6in tall; otherwise the main stem will shoot up towards the sky, producing a very leggy plant.

Growing conditions Full sun and moderately fertile, well-drained soil.

To feed or not to feed Not necessary.

Cosmos is a must for any cut flower patch and will attract bees and hoverflies from far and wide.

Height 45cm–1.5m/18in–5ft.
Spread 40cm/16in.
Spacing 40–45cm/16–18in.
Support Taller varieties will need support.
Recommended varieties 'Candy Stripe' – a white flower flushed with pale pink edges to the petals; 'Purity' – a pure white; 'Rubenza' – a dark pink/crimson colour, grows to 75cm/30in.
When to pick As petals start to unfurl.
Conditioning Leave for several hours or overnight in deep buckets of water before arranging.

Blue lace flower

I love this unusual, eye-catching flower from Australia, with its tightly packed umbels of pale blue/lilac flowers forming a pretty dome, like a chunkier wild carrot (*Daucus carota*) or cow parsley (*Anthricus sylvestris*). It can be a little difficult to germinate, taking 3–4 weeks, and germination is erratic, with some seeds appearing quickly and others taking much longer. They are worth it though. Once established on your cut flower patch they will flower for more than three months. The plant itself is open and quite sprawling. I tend to plant them close together so that their branches intertwine; also plants take up less space this way. Hoverflies adore their flowers.

When to sow Indoors in early spring.
Plant out Plant out after last frost.
Flowers Midsummer through to autumn.
Pinching out Not necessary.
Growing conditions Full sun and well-drained soil.
To feed or not to feed Well-rotted compost incorporated into soil in spring.
Height 45cm/18in.

Common name **Blue lace flower**
Latin name *Trachymene coerulea,* **syn.** *Didiscus coeruleus*
Family **Apiaceae**
Half-hardy annual
Why grow it? **Delicate flowers loved by hoverflies**

Blue lace flower is a little hard to grow from seed, but persevere and you will be rewarded with exquisite flowers.

Spread 30–35cm/12–14in.
Spacing 30cm/12in.
Support Not necessary.
Recommended varieties 'Blue Lace'; 'Lacy Series Mixed' for a mix of whites, pinks and lilacs.
When to pick When a quarter of the flowers on the head have opened.
Conditioning Place in deep cold water up to the flower head for several hours or overnight before arranging.

Black-eyed Susan

This is a wild flower from North America used by the native population in herbal medicine. It is an invaluable addition to the cutting patch, providing colourful flowers to pick in late summer and into autumn. Just like other members of the aster family, black-eyed Susan flowers each have a circle of petals with a central area made up of tiny true flowers. In black-eyed Susan this centre is a prominent central cone that is often black. Because the actual flowers are so small, members of the aster family have evolved the outer colourful petals to attract pollinators to the central flowers. The 'hirta' part of the name is from the Latin *hirsuta*, meaning hairy, and refers to the stems, leaves and bracts, which are all covered in tiny hairs – giving the plant a rough feel. The hairs can cause skin allergies so you may want to wear gloves when handling the flowers. Its stiff stems make black-eyed Susan perfect for cutting, and the flowers last more than a week in a vase.

Common name **Black-eyed Susan**
Latin name *Rudbeckia hirta*
Family **Asteraceae**
Half-hardy annual
Why grow it? **Late-flowering plants to brighten up your day. Butterflies love them too**

When to sow Indoors in early spring.
Plant out After the last frost.
Flowers Midsummer to autumn.
Pinching out Black-eyed Susan produces bushy plants, but if they look leggy pinch out when plants have five true leaves.
Growing conditions Full sun and moderately fertile, well-drained soil.
To feed or not to feed Not neccessary.
Height 60–70cm/24–28in.
Spread 40cm/16in.
Spacing 45cm/18in.
Support Not necessary.
Recommended varieties 'Cherry Brandy' – a red-coloured black-eyed Susan; 'Cappucino' – bronze-coloured petals fading to golden yellow at the tips; 'Prairie Sun' – unusual green cone and yellow petals.
When to pick Cut when the petals have unfurled but the central cone is still tight and the tiny flowers have yet to open.
Conditioning None needed.

Black-eyed Susans are easy-going plants that will flower well into autumn.

Statice

Statice has suffered from a reputation as a dusty dried flower, a stalwart of a certain type of tearoom, but its value as a fresh cut flower is being rediscovered. A Mediterranean plant, statice is related to sea lavender (*Limonium vulgare*), which can be found growing on salt marshes and around coastlines. The colourful papery parts of the flower are actually bracts (a type of leaf). Statice evolved these to attract pollinating insects to its otherwise insignificant flowers, which are especially popular with butterflies.

If you do want to dry some statice, pick it just before the actual flowers are fully open, since they will continue to develop during the drying process. Tie in a bunch and hang them upside down in a dry airy place, out of the sun. An airing cupboard is ideal. The colour will fade if they are dried in the sun.

When to sow Indoors from late winter to mid-spring.

Plant out After danger of frost has passed.

Flowers Midsummer from an early sowing.

Pinching out Not necessary.

Growing conditions Full sun; good drainage. They do well on sandy soils.

To feed or not to feed Not necessary.

Height 50cm/20in.

Spread 25cm/10in.

Spacing 30–35cm/12–14in.

Support Grow through pea netting.

Recommended varieties 'New Art Shades'; 'Sunburst Series Mixed'.

When to pick When the tiny actual flowers are visible within the bracts.

Conditioning Remove the green 'wings' running up the stem, wherever they will be under water.

Keep vases of dried flowers such as statice out of strong sunlight to preserve their colouring.

Although it is considered an old-fashioned plant I believe interest in statice as a cut flower is due for a revival.

Common name **Statice**

Latin name ***Limonium sinuatum***

Family **Plumbaginaceae**

Half-hardy annual

Why grow it? **Long-lasting flowers, which can also be dried**

Common name **Zinnia**

Latin name *Zinnia elegans*

Family **Asteraceae**

Half-hardy annual

Why grow it? **Cheerful colours into autumn**

Zinnia

Being a native of Mexico and surrounding countries, zinnia is probably the most temperamental and difficult to grow of all the plants I am recommending. It can struggle in a cool-temperate climate because it thrives in warm sunshine and dislikes wet weather. Zinnias are such pretty flowers and given the right conditions will produce buckets full of flowers. They come in a range of rich, bright cheerful colours – these are bold and some might say a little brash. I have a bit of a love–hate relationship with zinnias. I could not imagine doing without them on my cutting patch each year, but I get frustrated when they fail to perform. Commercial flower growers often plant them in polytunnels, thereby eliminating the worst of the weather, but if you are growing on a small scale this is not an option. In damp wet areas, zinnias perform in some years but not others, but you may have more luck if you live in a drier, warmer place. I persevere with them simply because when they do work they are worth it. My concession is to devote just a little space to them. That way if I do not get much of a crop I will have plenty of other flowers to pick from instead.

The other key to improving your success rate with zinnias is in the choice of variety you grow. Some are much fussier and harder to cultivate than others. The lime-green flowering varieties such as 'Envy' can be very difficult, which is disappointing as the flowers are stunning. I have had greatest success with 'Sprite Mixed', which includes a selection of bright pinks, oranges and crimson flowers. They are very easy to get to germinate and can appear just a few days after sowing, which always takes me by surprise no matter how many times I grow them. They do not like root disturbance though, and it is best not to sow them directly into the soil as it is unlikely the ground will be warm enough until quite late into the season, when it will be a race against time for them to put on enough growth to flower. The only way to grow zinnias is to sow into module trays or small individual pots. Sow a few per pot and then remove any surplus seedlings to leave one to grow on strongly. Do not allow the young plants to become pot-bound, so pot on frequently at the first sign of roots appearing from the base of your pots.

When to sow Mid-spring.

Plant out After last frost.

Flowers Late summer to mid-autumn.

Pinching out When the plants have four true leaves.

Growing conditions Full sun and well-drained soil.

To feed or not to feed A comfrey feed once flowering will encourage more blooms.

Height 45–80cm/18–32in.

Spread 40cm/16in.

Spacing 45cm/18in.

Support Taller varieties will benefit from being grown through pea netting.

Recommended varieties 'Sprite Mixed'; 'Giant Dahlia Mix'.

When to pick When petals have fully opened but centre is still tight.

Conditioning Remove all leaves as these will draw water away from the flower. Leave in deep water for several hours or overnight before arranging.

The rich vibrant colours of zinnias are a welcome sight in autumn.

Snapdragon

These are plants that make me think of my childhood, when I was endlessly fascinated once I realised that, by pinching the sides, a flower would open and close, as if it were trying to do a fish impression.

Tall spires of flowers emerge from a clump of leaves, with the individual blooms that run the length of each stem opening from the bottom up. In the height of summer, as I am bent down weeding or picking flowers, I love to hear the frantic buzzing of a bumble bee as it pushes open the two lips of the flower and crawls inside to the nectary delight that awaits.

Snapdragons used to be a popular plant to grow in wall crevices in cottage gardens. Nowadays they are more popular as bedding plants, especially now that plant breeders are producing dwarf varieties. These new flowers are often doubles with frilly petals. For me they have lost the charm of their taller simpler parents, which are now difficult to source in garden centres and nurseries. Seeds are still available though, and it is the taller varieties that you need to grow if you want cut flowers.

Snapdragons are tender perennials. They can occasionally survive a mild winter in cool-temperate climates, but the plant can become scrawny, woody and not especially floriferous. It is much better to treat them as half-hardy annuals, but give them a long growing season by sowing them early, indoors in late winter.

When to sow Indoors in late winter or early spring on to the surface of moist potting compost; do not cover.

Plant out Late spring.

Flowers Early summer to mid-autumn.

Pinching out Remove the growing tips when they have four sets of true leaves.

Growing conditions Sun and well-drained soil.

To feed or not to feed Dig compost into the soil in autumn or spring.

Height 45–75cm/18–30in.

Spread 35cm/14in.

Spacing 40cm/16in.

Support Taller varieties with pea netting.

Recommended varieties 'Night and Day' – a bicoloured, dark red and white; 'Rocket Mixed' produce tall sturdy stems and come in a range of colours from yellow and orange to pink and purple; 'Royal Bride' – one of a new group of scented snapdragons.

When to pick When one-third of the flowers are open.

Conditioning In tepid water for a few hours.

Snapdragon flower spikes add height and structure to your flower arrangements.

Common name **Snapdragon**
Latin name *Antirrhinum majus*
Family **Plantaginaceae**
Short-lived perennial/half-hardy annual
Why grow it? **Spires of flowers, which
add height to arrangements**

Common name **Stock**
Latin name *Matthiola incana*
Family **Brassicaceae**
Biennial
Why grow it? **Beautiful scent and
long-lasting flowers**

Biennials

Stock

Stocks are one of my favourite flowers. I will admit there are more attractive flowers out there, but once you have smelt a bunch of stocks you will understand why I love them so much. Their heady perfume is stronger than any sweet pea and, unlike sweet peas, whose flowers and scent fade after only a couple of days, stocks will go on filling your room with their fragrance for well over a week.

Stocks were known by Elizabethans as gillyflowers, a name given to several different plants including sweet Williams (*Dianthus barbatus*), which shared a fragrance similar to cloves. It is believed the name derives from the old French word for cloves, *girofle*. They were also very popular with the Victorians but seem to have fallen out of favour with modern gardeners. Two types of *Matthiola incana* make good additions to the cutting patch: 'Ten-week stocks' (which refers to the time it takes from sowing for them to flower) and 'Brompton Mixed'. The former are grown as annuals and have fancier flowers with a greater variety of colours, but they produce only single stems, so once picked there will be no more. Then there are the biennials, which are often referred to as 'Brompton Mixed'. The advantage of these is that they are sown in summer one year, they overwinter and then flower in early spring the following year, providing bunches of fragrant flowers when the cutting garden might

otherwise be quite bare. They form branched plants, so you can pick for several months. When they finish flowering in early summer they can be dug up, composted and their space filled with later-flowering plants such as dahlias.

When to sow Early to midsummer for biennials. Mid- to late spring for annuals.

Plant out Early autumn for biennials; late spring/early summer for annuals.

Flowers Mid-spring to early summer for biennials; summer for annuals.

Pinching out Not needed.

Growing conditions Sheltered, sunny, well-drained spot. Prefers alkaline soils.

To feed or not to feed Well-rotted compost and a sprinkling of seaweed and lime feed in autumn. Scatter seaweed meal around the plants in spring.

Height 35cm/14in.

Spread 20cm/8in.

Spacing 25cm/10in.

Support Not necessary.

Recommended varieties Biennials – pure white 'Pillow Talk' and 'Brompton Mixed'; and annual 'Tall Clove Scented Mix'.

When to pick Pick when the first flowers on a stem have opened; the other buds will continue to develop once picked.

Conditioning Remove all leaves that will be below the waterline; these decay quickly, making the water slimy and smelly. Prefers cold water. Provided the water is changed frequently, stocks can last up to three weeks in a vase.

A posy of scented stocks by the bedside is one of life's simple pleasures.

Sweet William

Sweet Williams are short-lived perennials but are most often grown as biennials, since they tend to become woody and straggly as they age. Originally from southern Europe, they have been grown in Britain for hundreds of years and were recorded by the botanist John Gerard in his *Herball* of 1597. The 'sweet' refers to the clove-like scent, and it is believed that 'William' is a corruption of the French *oeillet*, which means 'little eye', referring to the flowers with their white centres. For productivity and vase life sweet Williams are one of the best cut flowers to grow, lasting up to two weeks in water.

Most sweet Williams are available in seed mixes, such as *Dianthus barbatus* 'Auricula-Eyed Mixed' with its colours ranging from white, pinks and reds to crimson. For single colour varieties look out for the dark chocolate-coloured flowers and foliage of 'Sooty', the vibrant pink 'Oeschberg' and 'Amazon Neon Purple', which has lovely dark foliage and magenta flowers. There is also a pure white variety, 'Alba', which the Duchess of Cambridge

Common name **Sweet William**
Latin name ***Dianthus barbatus***
Family **Caryophyllaceae**
Biennial
Why grow it? **Beautiful scent and long-lasting flowers**

had in her bridal bouquet. Plant breeders in recent years have created annual varieties – for example, 'Noverna Mix F1' – so if you miss sowing the biennial varieties the previous summer you can still have sweet Williams on your cutting patch by growing these annuals.

The flower stems of sweet Williams are initially quite thick and strong, and the flower heads substantial and bushy, but, as you pick them, the new flowers gradually become smaller and the stems thinner. They are still worth gathering – just be careful as the stems can be quite fragile. If you keep picking, sweet Williams will produce for three months.

When to sow Early to midsummer into trays or modules.
Plant out Early autumn.
Flowers Early to late summer.
Pinch out Not necessary.
Growing conditions Full sun and well-drained soil. Plant out in early autumn.
To feed or not to feed Well-rotted compost or mushroom compost in autumn. Apply seaweed and lime feed in spring.
Height 60cm/24in.
Spread 30cm/12in.
Spacing 30–40cm/12–16in.
Support Grow through pea netting.
Recommended varieties 'Sooty'; 'Auricula-Eyed Mixed'; 'Electron'; 'Alba'.
When to pick The flower heads are made up of tightly packed individual flowers. Pick when three or four have started to open.
Conditioning None needed.

LEFT Choosing my favourite cut flowers is hard but sweet Williams are certainly one of them.
RIGHT I love how the translucent, moon-like discs of honesty seed heads catch the light.

Honesty

You can grow honesty for its pretty flowers, which come in white or lilac-pink. The flowers have a subtle scent but they are not as floriferous as the very similar sweet rocket (*Hesperis matronalis*). They flower early, in late spring, which makes them a useful addition to your cutting patch, providing perfect filler material for arrangements with tulips. You can use the fresh green, oval seed pods in arrangements too. But it is for the silvery, ripe seed pods that most people really grow honesty. Gradually the green seed heads dry, turning brown and dull, and they look pretty uninspiring. It is easy at this stage to wonder why you bothered growing the plant.

Common name **Honesty**
Latin name *Lunaria annua*
Family **Brassicaceae**
Biennial
Why grow it? **Papery, moon-like
seed heads**

If left alone these outer casings naturally fall off, revealing a glistening interior. Meanwhile the seeds fall on to the ground. The delicate, paper-thin seed heads, known in some parts as moon pennies, can be easily damaged by the elements. If you have them growing in your garden and you want them to provide interest *in situ* over winter then you can leave them alone, but if you plan to use them indoors it is best to pick them when the seed pods are dry, but before the protective cases have fallen away. Each seed pod has a small spike at the bottom. Use this to peel apart the two outer covers, to reveal the shimmering translucent discs inside. Honesty seed heads look lovely arranged on their own in a vase or when mixed with grasses and other seed heads (see pages 194–7). I also like to use them as Christmas decorations. Tie a few small stems together with twine and hang from your Christmas tree where your lights will illuminate the seed pods and make them sparkle.

If space is tight I would recommend growing this only if you want the seed pods later in the year, as there are other plants which have more desirable flowers and higher yields. Having said that, only three or four plants will give you enough seed heads to decorate your home.

When to sow Early to midsummer.
Plant out Early autumn.
Flowers Late spring to midsummer the following year. The seed pods are ready for picking from late summer.
Pinching out Not necessary.
Growing conditions Happy in most soils and can cope with partial shade.

The white flowers of *Lunaria annua* var. *albiflora* capture the purity of spring.

To feed or not to feed Not necessary.
Height 80cm/32in.
Spread 30cm/12in.
Spacing 30–40cm/12–16in.
Support Not necessary.
Recommended varieties Flowers come in pink or white.
When to pick For the flowers, harvest when the first buds have opened. For the seed pods, wait until they have dried on the plant but before the outer casings have fallen.
Conditioning None needed.

Iceland poppy

Being native to areas near the polar regions of northern Europe and North America it is unsurprising that Iceland poppies are hardy plants which cope well in a typical cool-temperate climate in spring and summer. They are technically short-lived perennials but are often treated as biennials. The flowers are more robust than a lot of poppies, and yet they still have a delicacy about them. Crinkled like crushed silk, the petals come in a range of colours from pastels to more striking oranges, yellows and reds. The insides of the flowers are unmistakable, with the ring of anthers covered in pollen surrounding the stigma. Poppies are one of my favourite flowers so it is always a bit of a disappointment that most of them do not make good cut flowers. Imagine my delight then when I discovered that Iceland poppies manage to capture everything I love about poppies and that they last once cut.

When to sow Early to midsummer.
Plant out Best to keep in pots over winter in a cold frame or somewhere sheltered from the rain. Plant out in mid-spring.
Flowers Late spring to summer.

Pinching out Not necessary.

Growing conditions Dislikes very wet conditions and poorly drained soils, otherwise easy to cultivate.

To feed or not to feed Plant into soil improved with compost.

Height 30cm/12in.

Spread 20cm/8in.

Spacing 25–30cm/10–12in.

Support Not necessary.

Common name **Iceland poppy**

Latin name ***Papaver nudicaule***

Family **Papaveraceae**

Biennial/Short-lived perennial

Why grow it? **Delicate-looking flowers that you will not be able to buy**

Recommended varieties 'Party Fun', 'Meadow Pastels' and 'Illumination' for the longest stems.

When to pick When the floral casing has started to split and the first petals are visible. You can gently pull away the casings as the buds start to open.

Conditioning Generally it is recommended that you sear the stems for 15–20 seconds in boiling water, being careful to protect each flower head from the steam, then arrange them in deep tepid water. However, I have found the flowers last fine without any extra conditioning.

Stunningly elegant Iceland poppy is particularly eye-catching when arranged with grasses, cornflowers and feverfew.

Wallflower

These form quite bushy clumps, although they tend to become quite woody at the base with age and also have a tendency to suffer from a disease called clubroot, so are best grown as biennials. The cultivated varieties derive from the native plants that grow in the rocky areas of the south-eastern Mediterranean.

Wallflowers are mainly grown for spring and summer bedding, but they can also make good cut flowers. They are one of the few biennials for sale as young plants from garden centres and nurseries, but the selection tends to be restricted to dwarf plants. If you grow your own from seed you can choose some of the taller varieties, which have longer stems for cut flowers. A good range of colours is available from deep rich reds and oranges through to pale yellow and creams.

When to sow Early to midsummer.
Plant out Early autumn.
Flowers Early spring to early summer in the following year.
Pinching out Not necessary.
Growing conditions Full sun and well-drained soil. From the brassica family, so prefers alkaline soil.
To feed or not to feed A seaweed/lime mix when planting out and then again in early spring.
Height 30–40cm/12–16in.
Spread 30cm/12in.
Spacing 35cm/14in.

Wallflowers are useful for creating a flowery haze in spring arrangements.

Support Not necessary.
Recommended varieties 'Ivory White'; 'Vulcan'; 'Blood Red'; 'Fair Lady Mixed'.
When to pick When the first flowers on stems have started to open.
Conditioning Stems can be seared in boiling water for 30 seconds to lengthen vase life.

Common name **Wallflower**
Latin name ***Erysimum cheiri***
Family **Brassicaceae**
Biennial/Short-lived perennial
Why grow it? **Beautiful scent early in the season**

Wedding
flowers

When the Duke and Duchess of Cambridge were married in April 2011, the green and white seasonal colour scheme was a stunning example of what could be achieved with locally grown cut flowers and foliage. A simple elegance was created using lily-of-the-valley (*Convallaria*) grown in Cornwall, pure white sweet William and hyacinths. Myrtle, which is symbolic of marriage, was picked from a plant in the grounds of Queen Victoria's home, Osborne House, on the Isle of Wight. The other floral decorations came from royal estate gardens at Windsor and Sandringham. With the clever use of seasonal flowers and plants in containers the royal florist, Shane Connolly, conjured up a celebration not just of a wedding but also of the British countryside, with blossom, lilac and even pot-grown trees adorning Westminster Abbey. You do not have to be royalty to achieve something that reflects the seasons and to include flowers that have personal meanings.

The cost of weddings has escalated in recent years, and flowers can be a significant part of this expense. There has also been a growth in interest in green and eco-weddings, with the bride and groom wanting their big day to have less of an environmental impact. Creating a cutting patch to grow your own flowers is a way of saving money and reducing the carbon footprint of your wedding. For a fraction of the cost you could use your cut flower patch

Your wedding flowers do not need to have a large carbon footprint. If you grow your own it will be kinder on the environment and you will have flowers that are special to you.

Growing flowers for a one-off event such as a wedding requires a different approach to your planting scheme.

Small jars and tins make quirky vases for your wedding decorations.

to grow seasonal flowers for your wedding day rather than having to rely on blooms that have been grown abroad. Of course organising a wedding can be stressful enough without growing all your own flowers as well, so this idea might not be for the faint-hearted. You need to be realistic about the flowers that you will be able to have and the style that you might create. If you like the idea of simple arrangements and a more natural style, then growing your own flowers should really suit you. Rather than taking on all the work yourself you could perhaps share the job of growing the flowers with friends and family or just cultivate enough for the venue and leave the bouquets to a local flower grower.

Rather than trying to get your cut flower patch to produce over as long a period as possible, the emphasis when growing flowers for a one-off event such as a wedding is all about targeting your growing to that one special day. The date of your planned wedding will be crucial. Fresh flowers will be available from mid-spring to mid-autumn. If your wedding is for later in the year you could grow lots of seed heads and grasses (see pages 194–7).

When space and time are both in short supply you could just grow your own flower petal confetti. Make up some simple paper cones for each guest, and on the morning of your wedding collect a mass of petals from roses in your garden and from flowers on your cutting patch, filling the paper cones. Larkspur, roses and love-in-a-mist are particularly brilliant for confetti because you can dry the individual petals in an airing cupboard and use them when the flowers are no longer in bloom.

Tips on growing your own wedding flowers

✿ Planning is essential. When you have settled on a date for the wedding (or other special occasion) check what will be in flower at that time. Do not try to get flowers to bloom when they would not normally do so as this requires time, expense and the right equipment, and without these your efforts are likely to end in disappointment.

✿ Select a theme, perhaps three or four colours that work well together. Or you could choose to go with a colourful mix of lots of different blooms.

✿ Choose to grow varieties that are scented. Very few flowers you can buy are perfumed. Scent really will give your flowers that special touch and wow your guests.

✿ Try to work out how many flowers you will need. Not an exact number but a rough idea. Where do you want to have your flowers? How many tables will there be and how many guests? Bear in mind how much growing space you have. A tiny patch in your garden will not supply enough flowers to decorate your venue but could produce enough for a bouquet.

✿ Include family and friends in your growing plans. Maybe you could create a network of people growing for you in their gardens and allotments.

✿ It is best to pick some flowers such as sweet peas and love-in-a-mist on the day. Pick them first thing and then leave them in water somewhere cool before arranging.

✿ Longer-lasting flowers can be picked up to two days before they are needed.

✿ Bouquets/posies can be made the day before the wedding and kept, in water, somewhere cool.

✿ Keep the flowers away from fruit and vegetables once they have been cut, so they do not speed up their inevitable death. You do not want to find your blooms have shed their petals on the morning of the wedding day.

✿ To keep down costs and create a simple relaxed feel, collect glass jars and use these as vases for table decorations.

✿ If you have got time, hone your growing skills the year before the special occasion.

✿ Have a back-up plan, because unexpected weather does have a habit of causing gardeners problems. Seek out local flower growers. Some now do pick-your-own days or will supply the flowers but leave you to do the arranging. You could perhaps use some of these to supplement your own cut flowers.

Give each guest some homemade petal confetti in a pretty cone.

Agrostis nebulosa, when mixed with lady's mantle and a dramatic chocolate-coloured cornflower, makes a striking buttonhole.

Using delicate grasses, scented foliage and even small succulents such as echeveria and houseleek (*Sempervivum*) for buttonholes will give your home-grown wedding flowers that special touch.

Pick delicate flowers for buttonholes so that they do not dominate and their tiny blooms can be appreciated up close.

Bulbs,
corms & tubers

Why choose bulbs?

Allium caeruleum, with its striking blue flowers, makes an unusual cut flower.

Bulbs are not the most obvious plants for your cutting patch. They tend to produce only one flower per bulb, and once that stem has finished flowering that is it for the year. It might seem an extravagance to grow them for cutting, but there are some great reasons for finding a spot for them on your cutting patch.

Corms and tubers are treated in a similar way to bulbs but, unlike daffodils (*Narcissus*) and tulips, one plant will often produce flowers in abundance over a long period. I have included growing tips for dahlias and anemones – two classic cut flowers – later on in the chapter.

The great thing about bulbs in particular is that they do not take up a lot of space, which means they can be squeezed into small areas and interplanted between other plants. The selection is vast, from the very earliest spring flowers such as snowdrops and daffodils, summer-flowering ornamental onions (*Allium*) and into autumn with scented gladioli (often known as acidantheras) and dramatic nerines.

The key to growing bulbs for cutting is to have a few of lots of different varieties. This way you will not end up with a glut of flowers in one go but will spread your pickings out over a much longer period.

The choice available as cut flowers from the supermarkets and florists is restricted compared with those you can grow yourself. When you buy bulbs from a specialist supplier you have many more varieties to select from and can keep costs down too.

If space and money are tight it makes sense to focus on spring bulbs because these will fill the gap before your annuals and biennials come into flower.

If you want to squeeze even more flowers into your cutting patch, summer bulbs will give you exotic-looking blooms. Why not try gladioli? They come with the baggage of being outdated and over the top – all frills and dubious colours – but do not let their reputation put you off; there are some stunning varieties available, providing you with tall spires of flowers in late summer. I love the deep, rich crimson of *Gladiolus* 'Espresso', the dark purple of 'Plum Tart' and the zingy green of 'Green Star'. If you are really not convinced by them, give the early-flowering and smaller varieties a go. The white-flowered 'The Bride' produces dainty and elegant flower spikes, and if left in the ground will bulk up over time. I have some planted in among a patch of lady's mantle (*Alchemilla mollis*), their white spears poking through the sea of greeny yellow froth over summer. Or why not try the *Gladiolus nanus* varieties for striking, pink and crimson flowers.

Foliage from your bulbs can pose a problem on the cutting patch. It is all too tempting once you have picked your blooms to want to get rid of the leaves left behind, but if you want your

CLOCKWISE FROM THE TOP:
a dahlia tuber, a bulb and a corm.
It is hard to imagine stunning
flowers can emerge from such
indistinguished material.

Tulipa 'Angélique' is one of my favourites. Its flowers, with their delicately ruffled petals, blushed with pink, have an air of romance about them.

beds with them, giving you the space to infill with other flowers. This works particularly well with smaller bulbs. If you are growing in raised beds the area at the edge tends to have good drainage, which is ideal for many bulbs. The other options are to lift your bulbs and either replant in autumn or treat them as annuals, lifting them as soon as you have picked the flowers, putting the bulb and foliage on the compost heap and buying new bulbs in autumn. Lifting works well for daffodils and tulips, but other bulbs – grape hyacinths and snowdrops for example – are best left in the ground where they will bulk up over time. Plant the latter around the edges of your cut flower beds or in an area for perennial planting, where they will not be disturbed.

bulbs to flower in subsequent years that foliage is vital. The nutrients and energy stored in the leaves are transferred to the bulb as the foliage withers, so that each bulb can form flowers the following year. Waiting 4–6 weeks for this to happen might not seem like the most efficient use of ground, but there are ways of including bulbs while maintaining a high-yielding cut flower patch. Smaller varieties of daffodils such as *Narcissus* 'February Gold' or 'Jack Snipe' produce less bulky foliage than some of the larger daffodils. Choosing early-flowering varieties will mean that their dying leaves will not linger into late spring, allowing you to plant out your annual cut flower plants, which you have been raising indoors. Rather than planting bulbs in blocks, you could edge your cut flower

Lifting and storing

As the foliage of your bulbs starts to turn yellow, it is worth giving the bulbs a feed every week with liquid seaweed fertiliser. Before the foliage dies back completely, carefully lift the bulbs, taking care not to damage them. Place them somewhere warm and moisture-free – a greenhouse or cold frame is perfect – until any remaining foliage has died. Snip this off above the neck of the bulb and brush off any soil. Remove any little bulbs, known as offsets, because this will improve the vigour of the larger bulb. Store bulbs in paper bags in a cool dry place until autumn, when they can be replanted. Remember to label the bags.

Bulbs

There is a huge variety of daffodils available to grow on your cutting patch. Good ones might include (top left) 'White Lion', 'Stanway', 'Silverwood' and (bottom left) 'Falconet', 'Actaea', 'Irish Minstrel'.

Daffodil

This is a classic cut flower and one of the few flower crops still grown on a large scale in the UK. For most of us, daffodils are synonymous with heralding spring, but in mild climates the earliest blooms are for sale in mid-autumn. When your own cut flower patch is no longer producing, there is no reason to resort to imported roses and lilies when locally grown daffodils can be delivered to your door, filling your home with their incredible perfume.

The choice of daffodil varieties is immense. There are more than 27,000 named varieties, although not all of these are still in cultivation. The RHS groups all daffodils into thirteen divisions based on flower form and genetic

background. Large-flowered and long-stemmed varieties are perfect for traditional arrangements, but smaller blooms can be more practical. A few small vases of *Narcissus* 'Jack Snipe', with its creamy white petals and yellow trumpets, would make a cute spring display. And some of the highly scented types are a must. They pack a punch, and only a few stems can fill a whole room with intoxicating perfume. My own favourites are 'Geranium' or 'Falconet'.

All parts of daffodils are toxic, and it has been known for the bulbs to be confused with onions, leading to accidental poisoning. It is worth bearing this in mind if you plan to grow them on an allotment. Handling the flowers

Plant your bulb at the correct depth with the pointed end facing upwards.

can also cause dermatitis, known as 'daffodil rash' by daffodil pickers, resulting in itchy, dry scaly skin where it has come into contact with the sap that oozes from the cut stems. You may want to wear gloves when picking, conditioning and arranging your daffodils. This leaking sap means that the flowers will also require some extra conditioning before they can be arranged (see page 146).

How to grow

Daffodils like a sunny spot but can be grown in partial shade. In early autumn plant the bulbs outdoors. A later planting time is possible, but daffodils do benefit from time in the ground in autumn as they start to grow straightaway, developing roots before winter sets in.

Plant in individual holes or trenches at three times the bulb depth, with the pointed end facing upwards. If you plan to lift the bulbs, plant them as close as possible to each other but so the bulbs do not touch. If you prefer to leave the daffodil bulbs in the ground, space them about 10cm/4in apart.

Then all you have to do is wait. Some of the earliest daffodils can flower in midwinter, and the latest up until late spring. Try to choose a selection that will flower over a long period and then you will have a succession of blooms to pick rather than a glut at any one time.

Recommended varieties

'Actaea' – Height 40cm/16in. A gorgeously scented variety from the Poeticus division. It has pristine white petals with a reddish orange, flattened central cup. Flowers in mid-spring.

'Falconet' – Height 40cm/16in. A Tazetta variety of daffodil with several flowers per stem and small yellow petals with an orange centre. Strongly fragrant. Flowers in mid-spring.

'Geranium' – Height 35cm/14in. A multiheaded variety with small white flowers and bright orange centres. Delicious scent. Flowers in late spring.

'Ice Follies' – Height 40cm/16in. Large flower heads with ivory petals and a pale lemony trumpet that fades to ivory too. Very long-lasting once cut and one of my favourites. Flowers in mid-spring.

This early-flowering Poeticus variety, *Narcissus* 'Actaea', has a lovely scent.

Tulip

Plant breeding has created many different varieties of tulips, although you would be forgiven for thinking this was not the case from the lack of choice when buying them as cut flowers. The reality is a painter's palette – from the most delicate of pastels to the richest of jewel-like colours. And rather than the plain, goblet-style flowers of petrol station forecourts and supermarkets, flower forms are as varied as their colouring: frilly, feathery-edged Parrot varieties; Viridifloras with green-streaked petals; or dreamily romantic, double-flowered versions that resemble peonies. Some bloom in early spring, but the main time for tulips is mid- to late spring. Perfect for filling the gap as daffodils fade and biennials are just coming into flower, they are definitely worth growing on your cutting patch.

Originating in the eastern Mediterranean, their ideal growing conditions are light, free-draining soil with cold winters and baking hot summers – not exactly the conditions found in cool-temperate climates. Incorporating grit into the soil where you plan to grow tulips will help, and so will growing them in raised beds, particularly if you garden on clay soil or suffer from drainage problems.

The varieties you cultivate can make a big difference if you want to treat your tulips as perennials. Darwin tulips are the most vigorous and reliable, producing good blooms in future years, but they are, for me, some of the least interesting varieties. Parrot tulips, on the other

Tulipa 'Verona' is a stunner as it fades from ivory-white to buttery yellow.

Cream-coloured *Tulipa* 'Verona' and pure white *T.* 'Purissima', arranged with white-flowered honesty and wallflowers, make a soft spring display.

hand, are much more glamorous but are the least reliable repeat-flowerers.

You can lift tulips or treat them as annuals. The latter may seem extravagant but it is possible to get packs of twenty-five bulbs for the same price as one bunch of shop-bought tulips. Growing them as annuals has the advantage of not needing to wait for the foliage to die down before you lift them, freeing up invaluable planting space much more quickly.

If you prefer to treat tulips as perennials – whether by lifting them or leaving them in the ground – you will need to wait for the foliage to die back. In this case, plan to cover the area where you grow your tulips with later-flowering

cut flowers such as dahlias and zinnias, which you can have growing in pots until the soil is free. Or you could use a dedicated bed for tulips in your vegetable garden and follow these bulbs with tender food crops such as sprawling squashes and courgettes.

How to grow

Unlike daffodils it is best to wait until late autumn to plant tulip bulbs. They do not form roots until the weather gets colder, and if planted earlier in autumn they will sit in the soil and be prone to slug attack and fungal diseases such as tulip fire. Incorporate some grit into the bottom of the planting holes and plant the bulbs at three times the depth of the bulb, pointed end facing upwards. If you plan to lift them you can plant really close together – just leave enough space so the bulbs do not touch. For a more permanent planting allow a gap of 10cm/4in between bulbs.

Cut tulip flowers require special conditioning (see page 148).

Recommended varieties

'Abu Hassan' – Height 50cm/20in. Flowers from mid- to late spring and has stunning, burnt umber-coloured petals with flashes of yellow.

'Angélique' – Height 45cm/18in. Flowers from early to late spring, bearing beautiful peony flowers in the most delicate of pinks.

'Apricot Beauty' – Height 45cm/18in. Flowers from early to mid-spring. A delicately

If you are going to grow your own tulips for cutting try some of the more unusual varieties, such as these: (back row from left to right) *T.* 'Abu Hassan, 'Ballerina', 'Artist'; and (front row from left to right) 'Rococo', 'Red Shine'.

coloured, pink flower with tinges of apricot to the petal edges.

'Artist' – Height 30cm/12in. Flowers in late spring. A Viridiflora tulip with salmon-pink petals and flashes of green.

'Ballerina' – Height 55cm/22in. Flowers early to late spring. A Lily-flowered tulip in orange with hints of red. Smells delightfully of orange jelly.

'Rococo' – Height 35cm/14in. Flowers from mid- to late spring. A flamboyant Parrot tulip with vibrant red flowers and frilly edges.

'Verona' – Height 35cm/14in. Flowers early to mid-spring. A scented double variety with creamy white petals that fade to buttery yellow. Very long-lasting flowers on the plant and once cut. I love it arranged with *Erysimum cheiri* 'Ivory White'.

Ornamental onion

Of all the bulbs, ornamental onions are the one I would recommend growing if space is tight. The ornamental varieties of the onion family take up very little space and are perfect for interplanting with biennials. The globes of starry flowers on long, smooth leafless stems make dramatic-looking cut flowers. Try *Allium hollandicum* 'Purple Sensation' or the intriguing *A. vineale* 'Hair' with its green, Medusa-like flower stalks shooting off in every direction. The gigantic heads of *A. cristophii* are spectacular arranged on their own, but are difficult to include in arrangements with other flowers because of their size.

Roundheaded leek (*A. sphaerocephalon*) is useful as a cut flower because it blooms later than other ornamental onions, appearing in midsummer. Its smaller and more oval-shaped flower heads give it its other common name of

Allium hollandicum 'Purple Sensation' is the classic ornamental onion.

Roundheaded leek flowers from early to midsummer and its comparatively small flower heads make it great for arranging.

drumstick allium. Although a beautiful crimson colour, the flowers are less dramatic than other ornamental onions but are much easier to arrange with other blooms.

You can pack a lot of ornamental onions into a small space, but if you are growing the larger-headed varieties you need to plant these farther apart so that the flowers have room to develop.

One of my own favourite ornamental onions is *A. caeruleum*, a small-headed variety with unusual, blue flower heads. I love it mixed with the pastels of my summer-flowering hardy annuals and biennials.

Ornamental onions send out foliage quite early in the year but this starts to die back as the flower stalk develops. By the time the flowers appear, the foliage looks quite scruffy. To hide this, plant bulbs among other plants –

sweet Williams (*Dianthus barbatus*) work well. As they are biennials, sweet Williams are planted out in early autumn, but being still quite small plants there is plenty of room to interplant them with ornamental onions. By spring the sweet Williams will cover the ornamental onion foliage and the flowers of both will mingle.

How to grow

In mid-autumn plant ornamental onions in fertile, well-drained soil in a sunny spot. Incorporating some grit into the area will help to improve drainage. Set them at three times the depth of the bulb, 8–10cm/3–4in apart, but give varieties with larger flower heads even more room. As a member of the onion family flowers may give off a pungent smell, especially when first cut. Replacing the vase water every day avoids a build-up of the smell.

Corms

Anemone coronaria

These herbaceous perennials grow from a tuberous root, called a corm, and are native to the Mediterranean, where they form spectacular carpets of colour. In parts of Israel red anemone flowers have become tourist attractions. Their place of origin gives an idea as to the growing conditions they prefer. Full sun and well-drained soils are the ideal. The corms have a tendency to rot if they sit in waterlogged soils, and very cold, wet winters can kill them off completely, which can make them tricky to grow in cool-temperate areas.

I still think *A. coronaria* is worth trying. They are such beauties with their poppy-like flowers in rich colours and, unlike other bulbs I have mentioned which produce only one or possibly two flower stems, these anemones will go on producing flowers over a couple of months. Another advantage of these anemones is that they do not have a specific planting time. You can do this job in spring, summer or early autumn, so you can enjoy flowers pretty much throughout the year. If you are lucky enough to have a polytunnel you can even have them flowering over winter.

The fading bloom of *Anemone coronaria* is still worth treasuring for a bit longer.

How to grow

For a few years I struggled on my wet soil to grow *A. coronaria*. It seemed to prefer my raised beds in the garden, where the soil drains more easily. In recent years I experimented by growing them in pots. I now plant up individual corms into 1-litre/5in pots in autumn in a mix of multipurpose compost and grit. The pots then spend the winter in a cold frame before I plant them out on to the cut flower patch in spring. Doing it this way does take up a lot of space though.

An alternative is to plant the corms directly into the ground in spring and early summer, when your soil should be drier. Plant 8cm/3in deep and 25cm/10in apart. A mulch with composted bark or leafmould in winter will help to protect corms from hard frosts.

Recommended varieties

'De Caen Mixed' – Height 30–40cm/12–16in. A mix of purples, whites, pinks and red that is widely available. For single varieties try specialist bulb companies.

'Die Braut' (syn. 'The Bride') – Height 40cm/16in. A pure white variety that would be great for weddings.

I love to use triteleia, with its starburst blooms, to line the edges of my cut flower beds.

'Mister Fokker' – Height 30–40cm/12–16in. A violet-blue colour.

'Sylphide' – Height 40cm/16in. A gorgeous rose-pink.

Triteleia laxa

You might be more familiar with this plant by the name *Brodiaea laxa* – the botanical powers that be have renamed it. Native to California where it is called the grassnut, it grows as a wild flower. Its corm produces a clump of strap-like leaves, but, as with ornamental onions, this foliage yellows and withers before the flowers emerge. These are clusters of blue starry blooms held on slender stems, and they make great cut flowers lasting well over a week. I love trileleia arranged with the grass *Agrostis nebulosa* and feverfew (*Tanacetum parthenium*), in small posies.

Triteleias reach about 40cm/16in tall and spread to only 10–15cm/4–6in so are perfect tucked along the edges of your cut flower beds. They need full sun and like well-drained soil, which means they can struggle in very cold, wet spells. Where I live, winters tend to be wet at the very least, so I plant the corms – a couple at a time – into 1-litre/5in pots in mid-autumn and then overwinter them in a cold frame. In mid-spring I plant them out on to the cutting patch. If you do plant direct, set the corms about 7cm/3in deep and 10cm/4in apart. If conditions are right they will be perennial.

Tubers

Dahlia

When you see a dry dusty clump of dahlia tubers it is hard to imagine that they will produce any sort of life, let alone a vibrant, highly floriferous plant that will provide masses of blooms in late summer and autumn.

A tender plant native to Mexico and Central America, it was first introduced into Europe by Spanish explorers. Dahlias proved very popular, and within a short space of time plant breeders had set about creating new cultivars. Unlike most plants, which have two sets of chromosomes, dahlias have eight, and it is this that hybridisers have been able to exploit. Today there are more than 1,500 different varieties and species registered with the National Dahlia Collection of the UK. The choice is daunting: from the rainbow of colours (deep rich crimsons, delicate lemons, vibrant oranges and pretty pinks) to the array of flower forms (whether spiky cactus types, exquisite peony varieties or those with petals packed tightly into balls).

Dahlias make stunning cut flowers, but not all varieties last as well as others once picked. Some drop their petals very quickly, while others last two or three days. However there is a range called 'Karma' that is bred specifically for the cut flower market, so the stems are longer and, more importantly, so is vase life – flowers last at least five days.

How to grow

Dahlias are super-easy to grow, but make sure you start off with healthy tubers by checking

Dahlia 'Karma Naomi' is one of a range of dahlias bred especially by Dutch flower growers to offer long-lasting cut flowers. I love the rich colours of this variety, which works well when contrasted with golden *Rudbeckia hirta* 'Prairie Sun'.

they are firm and there are no signs of mould or rot. Tubers look like fat fingers that dangle from a central piece, which was the base of last year's stem. They are available to buy from early spring and need to be protected from frost. You can start them off either indoors or in a cold frame in early spring, or else you can wait until late spring and plant them directly into the soil. Dahlias planted directly outdoors however will not flower till later in the summer.

I plant mine in early spring into large pots filled with multipurpose compost, placing them on a sunny windowsill. Keep the compost moist but not wet. By mid-spring you should start to see shoots appearing. At this stage dahlias are particularly vulnerable to slug attack, so if you are growing them in a cold frame or direct into the ground you need to provide some protection (see pages 135–6).

Once your dahlias are growing well, start to feed with a liquid seaweed fertiliser every week or so. When the plants reach about 40cm/16in in height pinch out the growing tips to encourage bushier shapes.

When all danger of frost has passed dahlias are ready to plant out on to the cut flower patch. They will also need some staking as they can form large plants (see pages 125–6).

You should get your first flowers in midsummer, and with regular feeding, watering and picking or deadheading dahlias will go on blooming until the first frosts.

Since they are tender, dahlia tubers are best lifted and stored over winter. Wait until the first frost has blackened the foliage, then carefully lift each plant, removing as much soil as possible from the tubers and roots. Cut back the stems to the crowns and then store upside down somewhere frost-free for a week or two. This will allow the tubers to dry. I wrap my tubers in newspaper and leave them in a cool dark cupboard in my house. You can also pack them in sand. The important thing is to keep them dry and protected from frost until spring.

Recommended varieties

From the 'Karma' range I love 'Karma Naomi', with its deep mahogany red flowers; 'Karma Choc' is a dark rich chocolate colour; 'Karma Pink Corona' is a cactus type with candy-pink flowers.

Dianthus barbatus 'Green Trick' and *Panicum elegans* 'Frosted Explosion' go well with salmon-coloured *Dahlia* 'Yvonne' and dark red *Dahlia* 'Night Queen'.

Foliage
& fillers

Herbs make an attractive and aromatic addition to arrangements. Try apple mint, Bowles's mint, rosemary, sage or scented geranium leaves.

Foliage
backdrops

Using foliage to create a backdrop for cut flowers is the classic way to construct a floral arrangement. Adding a touch of greenery has several purposes. Just as in the garden, green foliage provides a neutral base, allowing the flowers to shine. Generally, in nature, flowers grow alongside foliage, so adding greenery to a vase replicates this, and it is pleasing to the eye. It also introduces bulk to an arrangement, so you do not need to use as many of your precious blooms to create an impact.

Florists rely heavily on evergreen foliage. However creating a background when you are growing your own plants, and on a small scale, requires a different approach. Shrubs and trees can occupy a lot of space. You may have a few plants in your garden that can supply some greenery, but if you used these plants regularly you would not have much of them left by the end of the summer. The key is to be imaginative with your choice of plants that will form the basis for your arrangements.

Some flowers have pretty foliage in their own right. Cosmos and sweet Williams, for example, come with their own ready-made, green backgrounds. By leaving foliage on flower stems above the waterline of the vase, it is possible to have plenty of greenery without the need for any other foliage. I sometimes pick stems of cosmos that have no flower buds on them, purely for the feathery leaves.

Unopened buds of sunflowers (*Helianthus*) make an interesting addition to an arrangement.

Then there are herbs. Rosemary (*Rosmarinus*), mint (*Mentha*) and sage (*Salvia*) all look very pretty when used in small posies, adding a touch of scent. Herbs benefit from regular cutting and will produce new foliage all summer long.

I also love using the soft downy leaves of scented-leaf geranium (*Pelargonium*) in posies, and the flowers also last well when picked. They would work brilliantly in wedding bouquets and buttonholes, where the aroma would be released when the leaves were touched. There is an incredible array of scents: for example, rose-scented P. 'Attar of Roses'; and P. 'American Prince of Orange', which has citrus-scented leaves. Mint, apricot, lemon – you name it. There is even a variety that smells like cola-bottle sweets – possibly not one for the wedding bouquet though.

Fillers

You can also use material other than foliage to create a background to a cut flower arrangement. Such fillers are plant material that would be unremarkable if used on their own, but when mixed with other flowers they create the perfect foils. They can be unopened flower buds, green flowers, grasses or plants that produce masses of tiny flowers. Try using the unopened buds of the smaller varieties of sunflowers such as *Helianthus debilis* 'Vanilla Ice' or the tightly packed buds of scabious flowers. I have recently discovered the sweet William variety *Dianthus barbatus* 'Green

Trick'. Bred in Holland, it produces lime-green, fuzzy pom-poms, which are actually undeveloped flower buds. No flower means no seed, so 'Green Trick' can be reproduced only vegetatively and to grow this yourself you will have to buy in some plug plants. The sterility of the plant does mean the 'flowers' last for ages both on the plant and when cut, but it will not provide any nectar or pollen for pollinating insects. You can create a similar effect by using the spiky unopened buds of other sweet William varieties if you prefer.

The perennial lady's mantle produces soft hairy leaves scalloped around the edges. They unfurl to form a mound in mid-spring, when stems of tiny, star-like, acid-green flowers emerge. These provide such a great contrast

OPPOSITE, LEFT The green bracts of thorow-wax (*Bupleurum rotundifolium*)

OPPOSITE, RIGHT The loose erect flower heads of lady's mantle

ABOVE LEFT The frothy green umbels of dill (*Anethum graveolens*)

ABOVE RIGHT The green pom-pom flowers of *Dianthus barbatus* 'Green Trick'

to other hues, and the flowers are so small, that they create a haze of colour, which does not detract from the other larger flowers in the arrangement. Lady's mantle does tend to self-sow prolifically – so much so that some

When you grow herbs such as dill you not only have flavourings for the kitchen but cutting material too.

nurseries but it is such a common plant you are bound to know someone who has some of it in their garden and will be more than happy to give you a piece. Early spring and autumn are good times to divide lady's mantle to make new ones, and once you have some growing in your garden you will find little plants appearing around and about. Pot these seedlings on until they are good-sized plants, and then you can plant them out where you want them.

The advantage of growing lady's mantle as a cut flower is that, by picking the flowers, you curb its self-seeding tendencies. It blooms from late spring to midsummer, after which you can cut it right back to the base of the plant. This does look brutal, but in 10–14 days fresh new leaves will appear. Feed lady's mantle with liquid seaweed or comfrey for a second flush of flowers in late summer and autumn.

Some plants produce tiny flowers, but have bracts surrounding the actual flower, which are acid-green in colour and, in themselves, work just as well as any foliage. The annuals thorow-wax (*Bupleurum rotundifolium*) and eggleaf spurge (*Euphorbia oblongata*) are perfect examples of this, although both are problematic. *Bupleurum rotundifolium* 'Griffithii' is tricky to grow, having erratic germination. Plants are also short-lived and therefore successional sowing is needed to have a regular supply of stems. Eggleaf spurge, on the other hand, is easy to grow and will give a constant supply of greenery throughout summer. Its one downside is its milky sap, which oozes out when stems are cut or the plant damaged. It can be a skin irritant.

Gypsophila is the classic florist's filler. Its tiny white flowers on multibranching stems are perfect for creating a hazy, see-through effect. Growing it on a small-scale is difficult though.

people have been turned against this plant, considering it a weed. For me, a plant that can cope with most soil conditions, and pretty much whatever the weather throws at it, is an essential addition to any garden. Its long vase life and abundance of frothy flowers make it perfect for the cutting patch too. Lady's mantle is easily sourced from garden centres and plant

Lady's mantle is very easy to grow. Include some in your garden so you can pick it as a filler in many arrangements.

I tried it a few years ago and was disappointed at its short flowering period. You need to sow successionally every three weeks, which takes up a lot of space, and the plants just are not productive enough for a small cut flower patch. If you are growing for a one-off event such as a wedding, where gypsophila would look lovely, it is worth growing, but if high yields and a long-flowering period are your priorities then, in my opinion, there are other, much more useful fillers that you can grow. For example, wild carrot (*Daucus carota*) and ammi, whose flowers are small and not especially showy, create a lovely hazy feel in arrangements.

Of course not all your pickings will need any embellishment or backdrop. Some flowers stand out and work much more effectively when arranged on their own. Small stems of primroses and grape hyacinths would be overwhelmed by the addition of any extras.

Annual
fillers

Use fillers such as *Ammi visnaga* to bulk out your floral arrangements.

> Common name **Bishop's flower, Toothpick weed**
> Latin name **Ammi majus, A. visnaga**
> Family **Apiaceae**
> Hardy annual
> Why grow it? **Frothy white flowers for a naturalistic feel**

The best annual fillers you can grow on your cutting patch are the following.

Ammi

This is a relative of the wild carrot and native to Europe, Asia and North Africa.

The two varieties most commonly grown are bishop's flower (*A. majus*) and toothpick weed (*A. visnaga*), both of which produce white umbels similar to cow parsley. *Ammi majus* is more delicate, whereas *A. visnaga* has chunkier, thicker stems and bears similarly pretty flowers. Both plants have attractive, fern-like foliage and are loved by bees and hoverflies. I prefer to grow *A. visnaga* because I find it lasts longer once cut and does not shed its petals – unlike *A. majus*.

When to sow Indoors in early spring into modules. Outdoors in mid-spring.
Plant out Mid- to late spring.
Flowers Midsummer to mid-autumn.
Pinching out Not necessary.
Growing conditions Well-drained soil and full sun.
To feed or not to feed Not necessary.
Height 80cm/32in.
Spread 30cm/12in.
Spacing 30cm/12in.
Support Grow through pea netting.
Recommended varieties A. *majus* 'Graceland'; A. *visnaga*.

When to pick When one-quarter of the flowers on an umbel are open.

Conditioning None needed.

Wild carrot

This is actually a type of carrot. Most carrots are biennial, growing and developing the long taproots one year and then flowering the next. The advantage of the cut flower varieties is that they 'bolt' or flower easily, and earlier, so that from a spring sowing you will have flowers in the first year from midsummer up until the

I adore the plum-coloured umbel flowers of *Daucus carota* 'Black Knight'.

first frosts. Its tiny, star-like flowers are held in an umbel, but it is its colour that makes wild carrot such a dramatic addition to any vase. I just love its plum-coloured flowers, which are especially long-lasting once cut, and it is a very versatile bloom when arranged with other flowers. The flower colour works well with both

Common name **Wild carrot**
Latin name *Daucus carota*
Family **Apiaceae**
Hardy annual
Why grow it? **Incredible, long-lasting flowers in a stunning plum colour**

A pinky white, unnamed variety of wild carrot appeared on my cut flower patch.

pastels and the darker richer colours of late summer and autumn. Do not be tempted to eat the carrot root; it is not edible.

When to sow Indoors in late winter or early spring into modules or small pots to avoid root disturbance.
Plant out Mid- to late spring.
Flowers Midsummer to first frost.
Pinching out Not necessary.
Growing conditions Full sun and well-drained soil.
To feed or not to feed Not necessary.
Height Up to 1.25m/4ft.
Spread 25cm/10in.
Spacing 30cm/12in.

Support Grow through pea netting.
Recommended varieties 'Black Knight'; 'Dara'.
When to pick When the tiny flowers start to open.
Conditioning None needed.

Sweet rocket

This cottage garden favourite originated from the Mediterranean but can now be found growing in most temperate climates. Known by several different names, including dame's violet, summer lilac, night-scented gillyflower and queen's gillyflower, its four-petalled flowers look similar to those of stocks or edible rocket (*Eruca vesicaria* subsp. *sativa*). The heavily scented flowers of sweet rocket are at their most potent in the evening, hence their botanical name, *Hesperis matronalis*, *hesperos* being Greek for evening.

Sweet rocket produces a clump of dark green leaves at the base of the plant, before sending up long flower stalks. The leaves are lance-shaped with a slightly rough, hairy feel.

This fairly robust plant can cope with most conditions, which might explain its appearance in the wild, springing up in woodland and hedgerows. Being perennial, sweet rocket re-sprouts from the base in spring. However the plant tends to become very woody with age and produces fewer flowers, so it is best to treat sweet rocket as a biennial.

When to sow Early to midsummer.
Plant out Early autumn.
Flowers Late spring to late summer with a few stems into autumn.
Pinching out Not necessary.
Growing conditions Prefers full sun and well-drained soil but is tolerant of most conditions.

Common name **Sweet rocket**
Latin name *Hesperis matronalis*
Family **Brassicaceae**
Biennial/Short-lived perennial
Why grow it? **Sweet scent and long-lasting flowers**

I love the simple delicate beauty of the white sweet rocket, but the pink variety has a stronger perfume.

Recommended varieties Seed mixes are most common, offering a range of pink, lilac and mauve flowers. *Hesperis matronalis* var. *albiflora* is a pure white variety.
When to pick When the first flowers open.
Conditioning None needed.

To feed or not to feed Apply a mulch of compost in autumn or spring.
Height 80cm/32in.
Spread 30cm/12in.
Spacing 35–40cm/14–16cm.
Support Support with pea netting or canes and twine.

Spurge

The great advantage of spurge is that it is highly productive, but its disadvantage is its sap. This may irritate the skin, leading to sensitivity to sunlight, and the sap may also cause problems if it comes into contact with eyes. Gloves are recommended at all stages

The greeny yellow colouring of spurge bracts
make them excellent foils for other flowers.

when handling this plant. It also needs special
conditioning to last well in water (see page 149).

When to sow Indoors in late winter/early
spring. Outdoors in mid-spring.
Plant out Mid- to late spring.
Flowers Early summer through to first frosts.

Pinching out Not necessary.
Growing conditions Prefers full sun but will
cope with some shade.
To feed or not to feed Not necessary.
Height 60cm/24in.
Spread 40cm/16in.
Spacing 45–50cm/18–20in.
Support Grow through pea netting.
When to pick When yellow centres have opened.
Conditioning Sear stems in boiling water for
20–30 seconds to stop the flow of sap.

Greater quaking grass

This is super-easy to grow and a simple
addition to a cutting patch. Greater quaking
grass makes an unusual filler for arrangements
and will give your vases and posies a unique
feel. They are really versatile too. Pick and
use them straightaway, mixed with other
freshly cut flowers, or dry them for use later
in the year with other seed heads. I love the
iridescent, pearl-like quality of the flowers of
greater quaking grass, which catch the light,
dangling crystal-like from slender stems.

When to sow Indoors in early autumn/
early spring into modules. Outdoors
in mid-spring.
Plant out Mid- to late spring.
Flowers Early to late summer.
Pinching out Not necessary.
Growing conditions Full sun and well-drained
soil.
Height 40cm/16in.
Spread 20cm/8in.
Spacing 25cm/10in
Support None needed.
When to pick When flowers have formed but
are still tight.
Conditioning None needed.

Other grasses

I would also recommend *Agrostis nebulosa*, *Panicum elegans* 'Frosted Explosion' and squirrel tail grass (*Hordeum jubatum*). Agrostis and squirrel tail grass are hardy annuals and panicum is half-hardy.

When sowing grass seeds, sow three or four seeds to each module, but do not prick them out. Simply pot them on as a clump and then plant out. This will create good-sized clumps rather than spindly patches of grasses.

Agrostis and panicum produce plumes of flowers, which look like fireworks exploding, giving arrangements a hazy delicate feel. Squirrel tail grass sends out pinky-tinged, bushy flower heads, which look a little like squirrels' tails. Add a few grasses to your vases, especially if you entertain outdoors where the flower heads will capture any breeze, adding movement to your table decorations.

Seed sowing of *Panicum elegans* 'Frosted Explosion' is a must. This grass keeps on sending out flowers, and if dried it turns a dramatic, smoky grey colour.

Greater quaking grass is so easy to grow, and it can be used fresh or dried.

Making your
cutting patch

Start
growing

A windowsill is a great place to start off seeds. Turn trays and pots every day so that they receive an even amount of light.

Once you have selected the blooms you want in your cut flower patch you are ready to start growing them. This can be a little daunting at first if you are new to gardening, but it is worth remembering that the seeds inside the packets really want to germinate – you just need to give them a little help. For me this is one of the most satisfying parts of gardening. I must have sown thousands of seeds since I started growing, but the excitement at seeing the first tiny green shoots appearing from the compost never diminishes. So here is my guide from seed packet to cut flower patch.

Hardy annuals are indicated by the letters 'HA' on seed packets and in seed catalogues. These plants cope better with cooler temperatures than more tender ones, so can be sown from early to late spring. They will germinate more quickly, make larger plants sooner and be less prone to slug damage if you sow them indoors into seed trays or modules. But you can also sow them directly into the ground – just wait until the soil has warmed up. Old country lore demanded you test the temperature of the soil by sitting on it with a bare bottom. A more appropriate way, if you do not want a bad reputation with your neighbours, is to see if annual weeds have started to geminate. If it is warm enough for them it will be fine to sow your seeds. Certain hardy annuals can even be sown in early autumn to bear earlier flowers. Check the seed packet, as well as the recommended hardy annuals in this book (see pages 39–52), to see which are suitable. In very cold areas you need to protect plants in the ground and in pots from the worst of the winter weather. Cold frames and cloches have worked well for me, and so I get an early crop of cornflowers, scabious and larkspur.

Half-hardy annuals (HHA) are native to warmer climates and, as a result, need more heat in order to grow. They should also be protected from frost. Sowing them indoors in mid-spring gives them enough time to form good-sized plants before being moved outdoors. They can be planted outside from late spring onwards, once the danger of frost has passed. You can sow half-hardy annuals directly into soil but you should wait until late spring, and even then germination may be slow. The other disadvantage of sowing half-hardy annuals outdoors is that the growing season will be so much shorter, particularly if you are prone to early autumn frosts. Thus your plants may have only just got into their stride before they are cut back by the onset of colder weather.

Biennials (B) are often forgotten, which is a real shame as they produce some of the best, most productive and long-lasting cut flowers. They need to be sown in early or midsummer and then will flower the following spring. For me this is a great advantage. Earlier in the season there would not have been space for another plant on my windowsills and in my cold frame, but by midsummer there is plenty of room for a few more seed trays. Biennials germinate quickly in the warmth of summer. Prick them out and pot on, and other than watering when in growth they need very little attention until they are planted out into their final growing positions in early autumn.

By growing young plants indoors you can keep a close eye on them when they are at their most vulnerable.

Growing from seed

Optimum conditions

A seed contains a tiny embryonic plant that is just waiting to grow. In most cases all you need to do is give it oxygen, water, light and an appropriate temperature. Sometimes seeds require other treatments, but the seed-grown plants I have recommended for your cut flower patch are straightforward and easy to grow.

Seed compost gives your seeds the best start in life. It is specially blended, has a fine texture, is low in nutrients, absorbs the right amount of moisture and allows in oxygen.

You can use multipurpose compost when sowing seeds, but it is best to add perlite to improve drainage and air flow. Always try to source peat-free composts, since the use of peat in compost is damaging to important environmental habitats. Never use homemade compost for seed sowing, unless you are able to produce garden compost on a large scale, as it is unlikely to reach temperatures high enough to kill off weed seeds. This will make it difficult to distinguish between the seeds you have sown and any weeds that will germinate.

Plug plants

If seed sowing space is at a premium there are some companies that sell cut flower plug plants in spring, which you could buy instead, bypassing the seed-sowing and pricking-out stages. The size of the plug plant can vary quite a bit: from tiny little plants with just a few leaves to larger, more substantial, young plants. Plant them into small pots when you receive them and nurture them for a while somewhere protected from the cold. They will have been grown in warm greenhouses and will not take kindly to being exposed to the outdoors immediately. The selection of cut flower plug plants on offer is not as varied as the choice of seeds and often the quantities of small plants are much more than you will need for a small patch, but you could share any spares with fellow growers.

What you need for sowing

- ✿ Potting compost
- ✿ Perlite
- ✿ Vermiculite
- ✿ Seed trays
- ✿ Labels
- ✿ Pencil
- ✿ Watering can with fine rose

It is hard to imagine that in these teeny tiny seeds are the beginnings of a cut flower patch.

Warm up your compost

When you come to sow your first seeds of the year, potting compost stored in the shed or outside at a garden centre will be cold and even icy – and these are not the best sowing conditions for your seeds. Fill your pots and seed trays with compost but do not sow anything. Instead bring them indoors and put them on a sunny windowsill or near a radiator. After a week or so the compost will have warmed up, and it will be ready for you to sow in it.

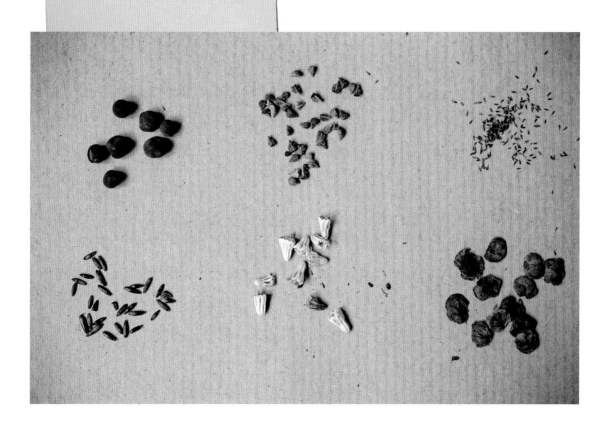

Containers

When it comes to selecting the right container for your compost and seeds there are a few factors to consider. Some seeds such as zinnias do not like root disturbance, so should be sown into modules or their own individual pots.

Whether you sow in traditional wooden seed trays, terracotta pots, typical plastic containers or recycle your own yogurt pots is up to you. I like to use small trays that come with a propagator lid or half-sized seed trays. Both fit easily on my windowsills, which means I can sow many different varieties in a small space.

Drainage holes are essential in any container for seed growing, otherwise your seeds will sit in waterlogged compost and rot. There is also no point in using deep containers unless you are sowing large seeds (see box, right). Smaller seeds will not have long root systems initially so all that compost will be wasted.

Autumn-sown hardy annuals such as larkspur can be started off indoors on a windowsill.

Sowing depths

- **Large seeds** such as those of sweet peas should be sown into large pots and buried about 1cm/½in deep. As these seeds will stay in their pots for a long period of time it is best to use multipurpose compost.
- **Medium-sized seeds** such as those of sweet William and honesty can be sown on to the surface of the compost and lightly covered with a fine layer of compost, vermiculite or grit.
- **Tiny seeds** such as those of snapdragons or crab grass (*Panicum*) are almost like dust. Sow these on to the surface of the compost but you do not need to cover them.

Sowing seed

Mix your potting compost with perlite to open up its structure. This will improve drainage and allow air into the compost, which encourages good germination.

Fill your container of choice to just under the rim to allow a gap for watering the compost.

Tamp down the compost to give an even surface on which to sow. For this I use the bottom of another seed tray.

Sow your seeds thinly and evenly. It is tempting to sow thickly, but the seedlings will then crowd each other out. This will result in weak spindly growth.

Cover medium-sized and large seeds with a layer of potting compost. Small seeds can be left uncovered. Label your tray with the name of the seed and the date of sowing.

Water the seeds gently, so you do not disturb them. You can use a fine rose on a watering can or place the seed tray in a container filled with water so it absorbs water from below.

Caring for seedlings

If you have gone to all the trouble of sowing your seeds evenly, be careful not to douse them with a jet of water from a hose or a torrent from a large watering can. You will just end up dislodging them and disturbing the potting compost. A small watering can – the sort you would use to water house plants – is what you need. This will have a much narrower spout than a garden watering can and will deliver water much more gently. Even better is a can with a fine rose attachment, which will lightly sprinkle water over your newly sown seeds.

Always use tap water for seeds and seedlings. Rainwater in your water butt could be contaminated with diseases, which can cause seedlings to die. Tepid water will make a big difference too, encouraging young plants to grow quickly, rather than sulking in cold compost.

Propagator lids, plastic food bags or even a see-through shower cap over your seed trays can be used to keep moisture in the potting compost. As soon as you see signs of germination, remove them; too much humidity can lead to fungal diseases.

Mulching with a layer of compost after you have watered will help to retain moisture in the soil. This is particularly useful in dry or windy conditions, when moisture may be lost from the soil more quickly. Use compost or even grass clippings left from mowing the lawn.

Pricking out

This is the gardening term for moving young seedlings, from the seed trays or pots in which they were sown, into individual containers so that they have the space and nutrients to grow into healthy plants. When your seeds first germinate they produce a set of leaves known as seed leaves. These allow the plant to start to harness the energy of the sun and produce food. The seed leaves differ from the plant's 'true' (or main) leaves. When these first true leaves appear it is time to prick out the seedlings.

Gently lift each seedling out of the compost, by its seed leaves. Use a plant label or pencil to lever the roots from the compost. Take your time, being careful not damage the roots.

The reason you should always hold a young plant by its seed leaves is that it will not matter if these are damaged at this stage.

Pot on each seedling into individual pots filled with multipurpose compost. Water, label and place somewhere warm, sunny and protected from frost.

Potting on and hardening off

Keep checking your young plants. When roots start to appear from the bottoms of the pots it is time to move them into bigger containers or plant them out.

Plants that are left in a pot for too long before potting on or planting out become pot-bound, which will hamper further growth.

From pricking out, it should be 6–8 weeks before your plants are large and robust enough to plant out on to the cut flower patch. Meanwhile check the bottoms of the pots every now and again. If you see roots poking through, pot on the plants into slightly bigger pots if they are not yet ready to go outside. A few weeks before planting out, the plants will need hardening off – acclimatising them to outdoor growing. Such hardening off is a gradual process, done by putting plants outside during the day but bringing them undercover at night for a week or so. Then leave them out overnight, perhaps with a covering of horticultural fleece. After another week the plants should be ready to be planted out on to the plot. Half-hardy annuals and tender dahlias are most vulnerable at this stage so listen to weather forecasts for any predicted frosts and be prepared to bring them indoors.

Pinching out

Removing the growing tips of plants such as these sweet peas will encourage them to produce side shoots and form bushier habits.

Some plants have a tendency to shoot straight for the sky, producing spindly plants with only one stem. Apart from looking dreadful these are never going to be the most prolific of flowering plants. What you need is stockier plants with numerous stems, which will produce plenty of flowers. The way to achieve this is to pinch out the growing tips of the stems when they are about 10cm/4in tall or when they have four

or five sets of true leaves. With your fingers, simply remove the stem above the third or fourth pair of leaves.

Sweet peas, snapdragons and zinnias require pinching out, while ammi and wild carrot are among cut flowers that can be left to grow naturally. See each recommended cut flower entry for details of whether to pinch out or not.

Cornflowers are one of the plants on your cutting patch that will benefit from pinching out, to encourage more flowers.

Planting out

By late spring you should have the first of your plants ready to go out on to the cutting patch. This final stage will allow them to get established quickly, and the sooner they are happy and growing well, the sooner you will have some flowers.

When trying to work out spacings for my cut flower plants I use my trowel as a measuring tool. I know it is 30cm/12in long and that the handle is about 15cm/6in in length. I then refer to these two measurements to give me a rough guide when planting out.

Extra food

Most cut flowers do not need a lot of nutrients. Too rich a soil will encourage leafy growth and fewer flowers. There are a few plants however that will benefit from some extra food.

For sweet peas and sunflowers I put a handful of comfrey pellets into the planting hole when planting out. Comfrey is particularly high in potassium, the nutrient essential for flower production and will give your plants a boost as it breaks down in the soil.

Dahlias are especially hungry plants so I add some compost or well-rotted manure to the area where they will grow, as well as a handful of comfrey pellets in the planting hole.

Sweet peas benefit from a handful of comfrey pellets placed at the bottom of each hole at the time of planting out.

Sowing directly

Some seeds can easily be sown straight into the ground. In some ways this is less time-consuming than sowing indoors and is a viable option if you do not have space for all of those seed trays. There are downsides though.

Your seeds and young plants are exposed to the vagaries of the weather. If the conditions are too wet, the seeds may rot in the soil. If it is too dry, you will need to keep the ground moist with regular watering. Weeding is important as weeds will rapidly colonise your soil, out-competing your seedlings for water and nutrients. Finally there are slugs and snails waiting in the wings for a tasty gourmet dinner of young cut flower plants.

Seed sowing direct

Use a fork to loosen the soil. Then rake the soil to break down any clumps.

With the end of the rake, mark out a drill in which to sow.

Water the drill before sowing, to create a moist seedbed.

Sow thinly and evenly along the drill. Do not worry too much about their spacing because you can thin them out as the seeds germinate.

Use the back of the rake to draw the soil back over your seeds. Label the row and water again if conditions are dry.

Seeds that are good for direct sowing

- ✿ Poppies (*Papaver*)
- ✿ Cornflowers (*Centaurea cyanus*)
- ✿ Love-in-a-mist (*Nigella damascena*)
- ✿ Grasses

Preparing the soil well is important if you are going to sow outdoors.

Caring for
your patch

Good maintenance

The final stage to achieving a blossoming cut flower patch is following a good maintenance routine. I know the word 'maintenance' sounds as if I am going to suggest months of hard work and toil, but nurturing your blooms need not be a chore or onerous.

Little and often is the secret to keeping your cut flower patch blooming over a long period and staying on top of weeds and pests. Some jobs can even be done while you are picking your flowers, so there will be plenty of time to sit back and admire your hard work.

Support

Providing some form of support for your cut flowers is essential if your site is at all windy and if you grow tall plants such as sunflowers. However even if your cutting patch is sheltered I would still recommend it. Heavy summer downpours and gusty winds can cause a surprising amount of damage – flattening large swathes of your flowers and snapping stems. I used to support plants as they grew and started to become floppy, but I was often caught out by the weather or simply did not have time to rescue plants. Providing support from early on is the best strategy.

One of the simplest ways of doing this is with pea and bean netting placed horizontally across each bed at a height of about 45cm/18in above the ground. Knock some sturdy wooden posts into the ground at the corner of each

Growing flowers through taut pea netting is one of the easiest ways of providing support.

LEFT Insert coppiced poles around the edges of the bed, to hold up the netting.

bed and then stretch your netting over them. I add a few bamboo canes or coppiced poles at regular intervals along the beds, to which I tie in the netting to provide extra support. The netting looks a little unsightly at first but will be hidden once the plants start to grow up through it. It is such a simple job that does not take long to do, but it makes such a difference.

If you do not want to use plastic netting or if the cutting patch is quite visible in your garden and you prefer something that looks more pleasing to the eye, you can make a framework from bamboo canes or coppiced stems. Secure these tightly with twine to create a grid across your beds, again about 45cm/18in above the ground. Yet another alternative is to create a supporting mesh from twine strung diagonally across the bed and wrapped around canes or coppiced poles.

Some flowers benefit from extra support. Sunflowers are best secured to individual sturdy poles, which should go a good way into the ground so that only two-thirds of each pole is above the soil. Putting these supports in when you first plant out your sunflowers will look at little ridiculous at first – a 20cm/8in plant against a 1.25m/4ft post – but it is much easier to get the stake into the ground when the plant is young so that you do not damage its roots later on. Tie in the sunflowers with some twine as they grow.

Both cosmos and dahlias become substantial plants with tall stems that are prone to snapping, particularly in wind or under the weight of rain. I support both with sturdy posts inserted into the ground around them in a circle and regularly tie in stems as the season progresses.

Coppicing

Most of us probably use bamboo canes for plant supports in our garden, but there is a local alternative – coppiced stems. Coppicing is a traditional method of woodland management in which trees are carefully cut to the ground; the new stems are allowed to grow until they reach the appropriate size to be cut down again. The time between coppicing can vary greatly depending on the tree: 1–3 years for willow (*Salix*); 6–10 years for hazel (*Corylus*); and 25–30 for ash (*Fraxinus*).

The practice of coppicing is an excellent way to harvest wood without the need to replant, and it is also an incredibly successful method of managing the ecology of woodland habitats. Cutting down the trees allows light on to the woodland floor, encouraging bulbs and herbaceous plants to grow; this in turn supports a whole ecosystem of mammals, birds and invertebrates. As the stems from the coppiced stools grow, shade once again returns to the woodland, but somewhere else in the wood more coppicing is taking place, opening up another area for the cycle to start there. Unfortunately many countries lost their coppiced woodland in the twentieth century: for example, almost 90 per cent has been cleared in Britain.

There has been a resurgence in interest in recent years, and gardeners can play an important role by supporting this new generation of coppicers and buying hazel poles and pea sticks rather than bamboo canes. By creating a demand for coppiced products they will encourage more people to appreciate this ancient but incredibly effective tool of resource management.

Coppiced hazel looks so much more at home on my cut flower patch than imported bamboo.

I like to grow
several different
varieties of sweet
pea up each
hazel wigwam.

Sweet peas are traditionally grown up wigwams of canes. You could use bamboo, hazel or willow. The canes should be 2.5m/8ft tall with 60cm/24in pushed into the ground. Insert six canes in a circle with a diameter of 80cm/32in, pull the canes together at the top and secure tightly with twine.

Watering

When they are first planted in the cut flower patch, your plants are at their most vulnerable. It can take a while for them to put out new roots and become established. It is therefore very important to keep them well watered, especially if the weather is hot, sunny or windy, all of which will put new plants under stress.

It is always best to give your plants a good soak occasionally rather than following a little-and-often routine. The latter will not soak water deeply enough into the soil and any moisture tends to be lost to evaporation rather than being taken up by the plants. Water that penetrates farther down into the soil encourages deeper root systems to form, so they can cope much more effectively with drought. It takes much longer than you might think for water to soak down into the soil. To test this you can dig a small hole in an area you have just watered to see how far down any moisture has reached.

The best times to water are early in the morning or evening, since less water is lost by evaporation. I prefer to give my flowers a drink first thing in the morning so the soil is not wet at night, which encourages slugs. Always water around the bases of your plants,

Nutrients

- **Nitrogen** (N) – for leafy green growth
- **Phosphorous** (P) – for healthy roots and shoots
- **Potassium** (K) – for flowers and fruit and for promoting plant hardiness

Comfrey fertiliser may smell revolting, but it does wonders for your flowering plants.

because directing it to where it is needed is the most efficient use of water. If you spray it on to foliage you are likely to encourage fungal diseases to infect your plants.

Feeding

Dahlias, sweet peas and sunflowers put on a lot of growth and produce huge numbers of flowers over the course of the summer. To help them to bloom so prolifically they all benefit from extra fertiliser every week or so. A liquid feed of comfrey (*Symphytum*) is perfect.

Comfrey

Comfrey is especially useful for a cut flower patch as it is particularly rich in potassium. The plant develops long taproots, which grow deep down into the soil, searching for nutrients and minerals. Its ability to put on lots of growth throughout the summer means you can cut back comfrey leaves several times over the growing season, and within weeks it will have re-sprouted. Wear gloves when you are picking comfrey – the leaves and stems are covered in tiny hairs which can cause skin irritation.

The leaves, packed full of goodness, can be used in several ways to feed your plants. They can be added straight to your compost heap. You can also use the leaves as a mulch, placing them around the base of your plants or in the planting hole where they will break down quickly. Another way is to make your own liquid fertiliser by stewing the leaves. It is really simple, but I have to warn you the smell is dreadful. All you need is a bucket, pack it full of comfrey leaves and then fill with water, keep it covered and leave for 2–4 weeks. Remove the slimy foliage and put this on your compost heap. Decant the liquid into plastic bottles; an old sieve comes in handy for this stage. Label the bottle and store in the shed. The liquid comfrey feed is highly concentrated so dilute it, one part comfrey to ten parts water, before using to feed your plants.

If you want to grow your own patch of comfrey, look out for *Symphytum × uplandicum* 'Bocking 14'. It is sterile so will not self-sow everywhere like the other varieties do. You will find it advertised for sale in spring in organic gardening magazines. Choose your comfrey patch carefully. Its long taproots are difficult to remove once the plant has become established.

If you cannot spare a dedicated area to grow comfrey, there is an alternative. You can buy comfrey pellets, which are made from the dried and compressed leaves of the plant. They are very easy to use. Just add them to planting holes or scatter them on the surface of the soil and dig them in. You can also steep them in a bucket of water to make a liquid feed, which has hardly any nasty smell, unlike your homemade brew.

Seaweed

Seaweed is amazing – it is so packed with nutrients that it is like a vitamin pill for plants. Not only is seaweed a good source of potassium (the nutrient essential for flower production) but it also contains other minerals and trace elements (nutrients plants need in only small amounts), so it encourages the growth of strong robust plants.

If you are lucky enough to live by the coast you can collect seaweed from above the high-tide mark for use on the garden. This would be good for areas where heavy-feeding plants such as sunflowers and dahlias are grown. You can spread it directly on your soil in autumn and winter or incorporate it into your compost heap. Before harvesting, you should always check who owns the beach and whether they mind. Also whether the beach is part of a nature reserve or Site of Special Scientific Interest.

Collecting seaweed is not an option for all of us, but dried seaweed in the form of seaweed meal and liquid seaweed fertiliser is readily available. Sprinkle seaweed meal on your soil in autumn and spring, and fork into the soil. The liquid feed can be used in two ways: simply watered on to the surface of the soil around your plants or as a foliar feed, sprayed or watered directly on to the foliage of your plants where it will be absorbed through the leaves. In both instances, dilute according to the instructions on the packaging.

Weeding

Inevitably you will need to do a certain amount of weed removal around your cut flowers. Weeds are not all bad though. Some are an excellent source of food for pollinating insects – a sign that your soil is fertile – and they are often packed with nutrients. With some careful treatment these nutrients can be harnessed and returned back to the soil.

The key to weeding is to understand a little about how they grow, which in turn will help you to keep on top of them. Some of them are even pretty enough to sneak their way into a few of my flower arrangements.

There are three types of weed: ephemerals, annuals and perennials.

Ephemeral weeds such as hairy bittercress (*Cardamine hirsuta*) have evolved to complete their life cycles in an incredibly short space of time, as little as six weeks in some cases, which

Put a lid on your stewing comfrey fertiliser. It will conceal the smell and stop rat-tailed maggots appearing in the liquid.

Keep the areas around your flowers weed-free but do not be too ruthless about weed removal. Leave some flowering weeds for bees and butterflies to enjoy. And why not pick some to include in your floral arrangements or as a posy?

means they can produce several generations in a year. If you ignore these weeds, they will quickly take over. The sole purpose of these weeds is to produce seeds rapidly.

Annual weeds, like chickweed (*Stellaria media*), complete their life cycles in a year. They die off in winter but their seeds remain in the ground ready to grow when conditions are right. If left to develop they will become more substantial plants than ephemerals. Both types are easily removed with regular hoeing.

It is **perennial weeds** that are the real problem. Some have evolved a two-pronged strategy to colonise your soil. The perfect example is dandelion (*Taraxacum officinale*). Not only does it send out copious amounts of seeds but it has also developed a more extensive root system than annual weeds, so it can survive winter underground to return again in spring. These roots often burrow deep in the soil, making them difficult to remove. As if that was not enough, dandelions can form new plants from the smallest piece of root left in the soil.

Perennial weeds are easiest to remove when small, before the roots have developed significantly. There are few things as satisfying to a gardener as pulling out a whole dandelion root completely intact, and few as disappointing as the all-too-frequent snap, as some of the root is left behind.

Clearing the weeds from your cut flower patch in spring, combined with regular hoeing, should be sufficient to keep on top of problem weeds. The good news is that once your cut flowers are established they will provide some ground cover, excluding light from the soil and making it difficult for weeds to flourish.

Disposal of weeds

Weeds can be packed with minerals and nutrients, making them excellent additions to the compost heap, but there are a few things to bear in mind. Annual and ephemeral weeds can be added as long as they have not set seed. You can also dig them straight back into the soil, but they need to be completely buried. Perennial weeds such as dandelions and daisies (*Bellis perennis*) can be added to your compost as long as they have no seed heads and you are sure the plant is dead. Never put them on your heap as soon as you have dug them up, as they will grow within the compost.

To make sure weeds are dead, drown them by submerging the whole plant in a bucket of water for a few weeks, then add the sludgy remnants to the heap. The water left behind can be used as a liquid feed on your vegetable plants. The other option is to bake perennial weeds in the sun, letting them shrivel up before adding them to your compost heap.

There are some weeds such as ground elder (*Aegopodium podograria*) and bindweed (*Convolvulus arvensis*) that are best put in your green waste collection bin, where the higher temperatures of the commercial composting process will kill them.

Deadheading

Even if you are picking from your cutting patch on a regular basis it is unlikely you will remove all the flowers. To keep your plants producing new blooms over a long period of time it is important to prevent any of the flowers left on the plants from going to seed. Checking the plants every so often and deadheading will make a real difference to the quantities of flowers you can pick. Just cut off any dying flowers back to a leaf joint and new side shoots will appear.

Removing dead or dying flowers will encourage the production of many more blooms for you to enjoy.

Pests

Aphids, slugs and earwigs might well be pests to us humans but they are – just like other insects – part of the rich biodiversity of the planet and are an essential source of food for other insects and birds. Wipe out any pest completely and you upset a particular ecosystem, even if that space is just your garden or allotment. It is suggested that the mass use of pesticides in agriculture is one of the reasons why the number of farmland birds has declined so dramatically over the last thirty years. No insects for them to feed on means fewer birds. Of course I am not suggesting pests should be allowed to take over, but it is possible to achieve a balance.

Understanding a little about pests, their life cycles, what they feed on and whether they are nocturnal or not can help enormously in being able to control them, as can dealing with them in the early stages to keep on top of any potential problems. A good time to check for pests is while watering and picking your flowers.

Fortunately cut flowers tend to suffer from few pests, but the following are the most likely ones you will need to look out for.

Aphids

Aphids cause flower growers problems because they feed on the sap of plants, resulting in distorted buds and stems. These tiny green or black bugs also excrete a sticky substance, known as honeydew. This in turn attracts sooty moulds, which feed on the sugary discharge and create black patches on the plant. None of this is desirable when the appearance of your crop of flowers is important. Aphids also transmit viruses when they are feeding, although this is less of an issue when growing short-lived plants such as annuals; it is more of a problem for trees, shrubs and perennials.

Natural pest sprays

If a pest has got out of control, as a last resort you can use insecticidal soap sprays, which are approved for organic growing. The active ingredient of fatty acids works on contact with insects, and is most effective on soft-bodied ones such as aphids. Spray carefully, targeting the pests directly, to minimise any impact on beneficial insects and pollinators. It is always best to spray in the evening when bees are least likely to be flying. Only use in still weather to avoid the spray drifting. Once dry, the spray is no longer active.

The real problem with aphids is how rapidly they can reproduce. For most of the year only female aphids are produced, and these are born already pregnant with the next generation. This accounts for the rapid growth of aphid colonies. It is only towards the end of summer that male aphids are produced and eggs laid, which then overwinter and hatch in spring. Aphid biology and how aphids have evolved to ensure their survival are impressive, but come across an ailing plant covered in greenfly and it is hard to feel benevolent towards them.

Check regularly for aphids once you have planted out your young plants, particularly around the tips of stems and the undersides of leaves. The best and simplest method of controlling them is by squishing them between your fingers. Because you have used no chemicals in their control, other beneficial insects will take up residence. Ladybirds and their larvae are especially partial to dining on aphids. If you do come across large infestations you can use a hosepipe to blast the aphids off the plant or else apply a natural pest spray (see box, opposite).

Earwigs

The common name for this small brown insect with pincer-like appendages on its tail comes from the Old English for ear insect, and reflects the belief that earwigs burrowed into ears. They play an important part in the breakdown of plant debris and other organic matter in the garden, but it is their sideline in eating flowers that makes them less endearing. Although particularly known for eating dahlias, they will attack other flowers too. You know you have got an earwig problem when your flowers take on a shaggy shredded appearance.

Earwigs are generally nocturnal, and this can be an advantage when controlling them. The traditional way to deal with earwigs is to use upturned flower pots stuffed with straw and placed on top of canes inserted throughout the cut flower patch. This gives earwigs somewhere to hide during the day, when you can remove any you find and dispose of them.

Pollen beetles

These are tiny shiny black beetles, which are mainly a problem during late spring and summer. They feed on pollen but tend to do little actual damage. Pollen beetles may occasionally nibble unopened flower buds, but the main challenge for a flower grower is to avoid bringing them into the house on your cut flowers. If you live near fields of oilseed rape, which pollen beetles feed on before making their way to your cut flower patch, it might be worth covering your flower beds in a fine

Ladybirds are a gardener's friend. When you work with nature, creatures such as this will do your pest control for you.

mesh or fleece. Otherwise stand your buckets of picked flowers for an hour or so somewhere dark such as a shed, with the door open slightly. The beetles will be attracted by the light and fly off.

Slugs and snails

Undoubtedly the biggest pests of all are slugs and snails. Both creatures are essential to the biodiversity of an ecosystem, performing an incredibly important role, breaking down decaying plant debris lying around on the soil. This is of little consolation when you discover your newly germinated seedlings have been devoured overnight, or that the much anticipated first sweet pea has been thwarted by a slug. If only they stuck to eating plant debris, gardeners and slugs could exist in harmony. Instead it can at times feel like a constant battle.

The question most gardeners ask of other gardeners is how to control slugs without

Slugs and snails are the bane of gardeners' lives. Fortunately you do not need to resort to chemicals to control them.

the plant outside the plastic sleeve is touching the ground as these parts will not be protected.

You could lay rings of eggshells, bran, wood ash or grit around plants, thereby making the surface of the soil uncomfortable for slugs. The problem with this is one of scale. You will need a regular and large supply of these materials to go across your cut flower patch as they will break down and dissolve over time, becoming less effective.

Perhaps the best way to ensure your cut flowers are not decimated is to start them off under cover, so when you plant them out they are strong robust plants. Young seedlings are perfect slug and snail fodder so protect them when they are at their most vulnerable.

To use any of these methods for all your cut flowers is unrealistic, but you could certainly use one for a few particularly vulnerable plants, along with some other control methods mentioned below.

resorting to chemicals. There are numerous ways of trying to gain the upper hand, and no one method is sufficient on its own. The best approach is to find a combination of controls that works best for you and to try to keep on top of them, particularly at the start of the year.

Barriers and growing undercover

Creating a barrier around your plants is one method of controlling slugs and snails. Copper rings and cut-down plastic bottles can be used. Copper gives slugs a small electric shock as they pass over it, putting them off progressing any farther. It is an expensive option for a cut flower patch and is better used on a small scale, say around the base of your greenhouse staging. Plastic bottles have worked well for me in the past, especially with sunflowers. Create a raggedy edge at the top with scissors in case slugs make it that far. Make sure that none of

Nematodes

These are microscopic worms, which can be bought as a powder, diluted in water and watered on to your soil. The nematodes seek out slugs, burrow into them and then pass on bacteria which are deadly to the slug. You need to wait until the ground has warmed up in spring before using them, and they are effective for only 6–8 weeks, so a few applications are required over the summer. This does mean it can be expensive to treat even small areas. If you have a particularly bad slug problem they may be worth trying, to reduce numbers and bring them under control.

Pellets

'Organic' slug pellets contain iron phosphate rather than the chemicals metaldehyde or methiocarb, which are harmful to wildlife. The iron phosphate interferes with the digestive system of the slug, preventing it from eating and so causing its death. Organic pellets are safe to use around pets and wildlife, but use them sparingly to avoid a build-up of iron in the soil.

A tip I picked up is to start using slug pellets much earlier in the year than you would expect. Most of us start to scatter them once we see the first signs of attack. Instead spread them in early spring, and this will impact on the slugs emerging after winter. It is tempting, particularly if your slug problem is bad, to dose your garden liberally with pellets, but use only a small number, thinly spread out, because this is when they are most effective.

Even though I use the organic pellets, I still restrict their use to early in the season, to get plants through their most vulnerable stages. Once a plant is robust enough there should be no need to scatter them.

Wildlife

By creating a chemical-free cut flower patch, you encourage wildlife to make it their home. Not only is this immensely satisfying but there is also a knock-on effect – wildlife will want to do some of the pest control for you. When I first took on my allotment I could not understand why I was not plagued by slugs. I had just assumed that would be part of the package. Then one day while I was having a break from weeding I spotted a song thrush hopping around the flower beds and helping itself to slugs and snails. If we work with nature, it will work for us.

Torchlight patrols

Slugs and snails are most active at night, and one of the easiest and most effective ways to control their numbers is to hunt them out

Blackbirds and thrushes help in the battle against slugs and snails.

at twilight. All you need is a torch and your chosen means of disposal. A bucket of salty water is favoured by many, but the resulting slimy goo is unpleasant so have somewhere in mind for its disposal before you start your hunt. Likewise with beer traps. My own preferred method is scissors; snipping them in half. It is not pleasant and for a while I wrestled with my conscience. But one way or another I need to keep them under control, and this method is at least quick.

To ensure you can enjoy a healthy patch of wallflowers such as these, grow the young plants in pots until they have well-established root systems.

Diseases

Fortunately your annual cut flowers should not suffer too many diseases, but even so when you grow organically prevention is the best course of action. These are the diseases you are most likely to encounter.

Powdery mildew

This fungal disease looks like a white dusty coating on the leaves and stems of your plants. My sweet peas normally suffer in late summer after several months of flowering. It is inevitable that plants prone to mildew will succumb towards the end of the season, when they are tired, but this disease can also occur when plants are lacking in water.

Make sure your flowers are well watered, directing water to the base of the plant rather than splashing the leaves, which will give fungal diseases the chance to thrive. Mulching with compost around the bases of plants after watering will help to retain moisture at the roots. Remove any leaves that show signs of infection, and feed with liquid seaweed fertiliser.

Rust

Snapdragons are prone to a fungal disease called rust. Tiny, brownish-orange spots appear on the undersides of infected leaves, which shrivel and die. Plants become weakened and generally look sickly. Unfortunately once rust has struck there is little you can do other than to remove any infected plants.

Rust is most prolific in damp weather. Look out for rust-resistant varieties and do not plant too close together, so there is plenty of room for air to circulate around each plant. Protect vulnerable plants from rain while ensuring that there is still good ventilation around them, to prevent a build-up of moist air.

Clubroot

Clubroot is mostly associated with vegetables from the brassica family, but it will also infect related plants that are grown purely for their flowers. In the case of your cut flower patch that means wallflowers, stocks, honesty and sweet rocket could all be vulnerable. Clubroot is caused by a slime mould that lives in the soil, and infected plants develop swollen distorted roots, which in turn lead to stunted top growth.

The most effective way to deal with clubroot in your soil is to grow any members of the brassica family in pots until they have developed strong healthy root systems before you plant them out. The infection can also be reduced by liming the soil. If your pH is 7 or over this will not be necessary, but if it is under pH7 a sprinkling of ground lime (also known as garden lime) will be beneficial. Application rates will vary according to the pH and type of your soil, so follow the instructions on the packet or consult an expert.

Crop rotation

Growing the same plants in the same area year after year can be one of the reasons for a build-up of pests and diseases in a garden or allotment. With vegetables the recommended rotation of crops is every four years. In some cases though infections such as clubroot can remain in the soil for up to twenty years, so moving your crops about every so often will do little to alleviate this particular problem.

On a small scale, crop rotation can be difficult, but it does not mean you have to move your cutting patch to a new site annually. Simply keep a record of what went where and move any brassica crops to a different area of the cutting patch, if possible every year. And for other flowers, move them every third or fourth year.

Cutting
time

Reap
the rewards

This is where you will start to reap the rewards for all your hard work. It is immensely satisfying to see buds starting to open on your cutting flowers. When you have put in hard work to get them to this stage it is worth treating your flowers with some care. At this point you have two aims: to remove the flowers from the plants in a way that will encourage further blooms to form; and to maximise the length of time your cut flowers will last in a vase.

More flowers

When cutting your flowers pick sufficient stem for it to be trimmed and arranged comfortably in your vase, but try not to remove the whole stem from the plant. You need to leave some of the plant so that new stems and flowers can develop.

Always cut a flower stem above a leaf joint because this is where new growth and flowers will form. If you cut midway down a stem it will die back to the leaf joint anyway and look unsightly. The one exception to this rule is Peruvian lilies (*Alstroemeria*). For this plant, remove the whole flower stem by using your fingers to twist and pull the stem away from the base of the plant, just as you would do with rhubarb stems. If you were to cut the Peruvian lily flowers, the plant would not receive the chemical signals necessary to encourage further flower stems to grow.

Tools for picking

Secateurs or flower snips are essential when gathering flowers. Secateurs are probably more versatile in the garden, being able to cope with more substantial stems. It is really a matter of

LEFT Deadhead your flowers regularly for a long season of blooms.

OPPOSITE To tie your flowers use natural products such as jute twine and raffia, which are compostable.

Place your cut flowers into a bucket of water as soon as you can after picking.

personal choice. I have a great pair of flower snips that cut through surprisingly chunky stems and twine, which makes them great multitaskers.

Whichever implement you use it is important to keep it clean and sharp. Sap from plants can be sticky and can build up on the blades of secateurs or snips. A rub with steel wool and a quick squirt and wipe with an alcohol hand spray will keep them clean, while a regular session with a steel will maintain the sharpness needed to cut through stems rather than crushing them to pieces. Stems absorb water much more easily through clean cuts.

You need to plunge your cut flower stems into water as soon as you pick them, so a couple of buckets are essential when harvesting. I use some old enamel buckets that I picked up cheaply from markets. I love the feel of the wooden handles when I carry them. I also have a couple of tall zinc florist's vases, which are useful for smaller flowers such as sweet peas.

Conditioning

This is the term used by florists to mean the steps taken to prepare a flower for arranging and to maximise the length of time your blooms will look good in a vase. Many imported flowers go through all sorts of chemical treatments and techniques in order to keep them fresher for longer, so they can be transported around the world and are still in a condition fit for sale when they make it to supermarkets and florists.

The benefit of growing your own flowers is that they could not be any fresher. There is no need to use chemical hormones to restrict blooms from fully opening or to put your flowers in a cold store for days to hold them

back. You can simply pick them as and when you want.

There are however a few tricks you can employ to ensure your cut flowers last as long as possible. When you remove flowers from a plant they are immediately put under stress. They will wilt quickly and, if not given the right care, will die.

The best time to cut your flowers is early morning or early evening. Plants naturally lose water through their leaves throughout the day, but this water loss, known as transpiration, is much greater in heat, strong sunshine and windy weather. Transpiration is at its lowest rate early and late in the day, and as a result your flowers will be under less stress if you pick them at these times. The reality though is that, with busy lives, sticking to this may not be possible.

It is also important to remember that growing your own flowers is meant to be fun and not a chore. I often end up picking my flowers at lunchtime since this is the most convenient time of the day for me. When I do, I make sure that once picked they go straight into a bucket of water and that I put the bucket in the coolest, shadiest part of the allotment while I finish gathering the other flowers. In summer, however, avoid picking in the middle of the day, when the sun is at its strongest.

Preparing your flowers

You can trim and arrange your flowers at once if you want, but ideally they will benefit from spending a few hours, or even the night, somewhere cool and out of direct sunlight – perhaps in a garage or shed plunged into buckets of water right up to the first flowers.

While preparing cut flowers, and once they have been arranged, do not place them near fruit and vegetables. This might seem a little

Make a clean angled cut at the base of each woody stem (1) and then a vertical cut upwards from the base (2). By creating such a large surface area through which the stem can absorb water its flowers and leaves will last well.

strange, but the reason behind this is the gas ethylene. Ethylene is released by fruit and vegetables as they ripen, and if they are near flowers the gas will speed up the decline of your flowers too. (It is the same reason why you put a banana in a drawer with your green tomatoes in order to ripen them.) Some flowers are much more sensitive than others, and it really can make a difference to the longevity of your floral arrangements.

Before arranging cut flowers in a vase you need to remove all the foliage that will be below the waterline and then trim the stems to the required length. Cut each stem at an angle. This exposes more of the stem and allows more water to be absorbed. It also means that the stem does not sit directly on the base of the vase, which would otherwise block the ability of the stem to take in water.

If you have quite thick, woody stems, say from shrubs or trees, the advice used to be that you

should crush the base of each stem. Although this is recommended widely, it does not help at all. By damaging the stem you actually make it harder for it to absorb water; you also introduce lots of plant debris into the vase, which is the perfect breeding ground for bacteria.

It is much better to make a wide-angled cut to the stem and then cut vertically about 2.5cm/1in up from the base of the stem. If flowers have been left for a while to condition they will need their stems retrimmed.

Using tepid water in your vases is preferable because it is more readily absorbed by flower stems. If you have arranged your flowers immediately after picking them, keep an eye on the water level in your vases, because flowers will absorb most water in the first few hours after cutting and the water will probably need topping up.

Most flowers do not require any special treatments, but the following are exceptions.

Daffodils

These exude a lot of sap when they are cut. If you were to arrange daffodils straightaway, this sap would block the bases of the stems and prevent water absorption, and if you were including other flowers it could be toxic to them. The sap is poisonous to humans if ingested and can cause severe skin irritation.

The best way to condition daffodils is to put them into a bucket of water for 5–10 minutes and refill with fresh water. Repeat until the sap stops leaking from the stems, and they can then be arranged as normal.

Daffodils look good arranged on their own but the addition of some zingy green young foliage can increase interest.

Tulips

These flowers are unusual as they continue to grow once cut. This does mean that as they develop they tend to flop and sprawl. Tulips will remain upright and rigid for longer if you wrap them in paper. You can use newspaper around the stems, secured tightly with rubber bands or string. Then place the wrapped tulips in a bucket of water for a couple of hours. Some people suggest piercing a part of the tulip behind the flower with a pin to stop the stems growing. I prefer to give them a bit of a trim every few days to maintain the desired height. I also quite like the sprawling effect of tulips spreading out from the vase like a Dutch master's painting.

You can help to keep tulip stems straight by wrapping them in newspaper, securing them with twine and plunging them in water for several hours before arranging.

Searing stems

Searing the stems of poppies, roses, euphorbias and dahlias in boiling water can prevent premature petal fall. Pick the flowers as normal, remove any unwanted foliage from the stems and then place the bottom few centimetres (inch) of stem in a jar of boiling water while protecting the flower from the steam.

Hold the stem in the water for twenty seconds before arranging in a vase.

Where to place your vase

Where you put your vase of flowers can make a big difference as to how long they last. A shady cool spot is preferable. Should you leave them on a hot and sunny windowsill in the height of summer they will wilt quite quickly.

Flower food

When you buy flowers they often come with a small sachet of flower food. This is a blend of sugars (to feed the flowers) and bacteria inhibitors (to prevent the stems from becoming furred up), and is designed to make your flowers last as long as possible. You can make your own version by adding a small amount of sugar and a dash of vinegar or bleach to the water in your vase. Personally I do not bother with all this because some flowers do not like additives in the water.

Refreshing the water in your vase every few days is the best way to prolong the life of your flowers. If you have time, re-cutting the stems at an angle will also help, exposing a fresh area of stem and improving water uptake.

Showing
off

A meadow feel to this arrangement was created using a combination of flowers and grasses from my cutting patch, as well as a few pretty grasses and weeds from the verge near my allotment.

Arranging
your flowers

At the end of the sixteenth century John Gerard was writing in his *Herball* about the types of flowers to use for 'decking up a house'. Over the following generations the taste in and style of floral arrangements have varied hugely. The rich, with the money, land and staff to grow vast amounts of flowers, were at the forefront of fashionable tastes. Huge elaborate designs in enormous vases would be popular for a period, and then – just as with taste for clothes and interior design – the desire for something simpler would emerge. Artworks of the day, from intricate embroideries to paintings, often captured the fashions and styles of cut flowers at that particular time.

Large still-life oil paintings of flowers arranged in vases show the reverence in which these blooms were held. For the upper classes the job of looking after and arranging the cut flowers was often done by the head gardener. With so many blooms in need of conditioning the big estate gardens would often have dedicated rooms in the outbuildings of the walled garden, where the flowers could be prepared before being taken to the house.

It was not just the upper classes that were fascinated by growing flowers for the home. By the nineteenth century, books and journals aimed at the emerging middle classes, with their suburban villas, were published.

As yet there were no florist's shops, and so

Arranging your home-grown cut flowers need not be time-consuming or scary.

you either grew your own flowers or bought them direct from growers or market traders. In fact the term 'florist' at that time meant something entirely different to its current usage. In the eighteenth and nineteenth centuries the word 'florist' referred to an amateur grower with an interest in a particular flower purely for its decorative beauty and the breeding and showing of it.

'Floristry' as it was known was particularly popular with men who worked from home: for example, in the UK the Lancashire weavers grew auriculas, and the Wakefield Tulip Society specialised in breeding tulips with beautiful feathered and striped markings on their petals. The florists' societies that were formed later became the horticultural societies, where showing was extended to fruit and vegetables. Towards the end of the nineteenth century the first people specialising in the sale of cut flowers from a shop adopted the term 'florist'.

The words 'flower arranging' can strike fear into many. For an amateur the idea that

there are so many rules and techniques can be quite daunting. I did once sign up to a flower arranging course at my local college. Then I happened to be walking past the classroom one day and saw a display of pristine, if a little artificial-looking, flowers and the tutor contorting some poor unsuspecting blooms into strange shapes. Needless to say I changed my mind about doing the course.

There is huge skill involved in creating elaborate bouquets, impressive centrepieces and the sort of designs on display in the marquees at shows such as the RHS Chelsea Flower Show, in London, UK. But most of us want much simpler arrangements in our own homes and do not have the time to spend primping and preening flowers. Some of the most straightforward arrangements can be among the most beautiful. A single stem of cherry (*Prunus*) blossom or a bunch of primroses looks stunning and requires hardly any effort at all on your part.

Simplicity is the key. Sometimes all that is needed is trimming the stems of your flowers to fit the vase and placing them in it. However if you want to create an arrangement of several different flowers, or you wish to arrange them for a special occasion, it does help to adopt a few simple tips to make the most of your blooms (see page 156).

Selecting a vase

Your choice of vase is crucial to showing off your flowers at their best. Building up a collection of containers that you can use is a good idea, as is seeking out new and unusual vases. They do not have to be expensive.

Use your imagination when it comes to what to put your flowers in. Although you may have a suitably tall plain glass vase in your home, there are so many other containers you could use that will add a touch of individuality and quirkiness to your display.

The only really essential requirement of a vase is that it is watertight. It is best not to pick something with a wide neck or one that is very big. It will take a considerable number of flowers to fill them, and they will be difficult to arrange and will tend to be quite floppy, because the container will not be able to provide enough support.

I love jugs. If you are at all nervous about creating your own arrangements in such a vessel, get yourself a few in different colours, sizes and styles. The reason jugs are so brilliant is that they naturally narrow towards the top and this creates an easy shape in which to arrange your flowers, with the neck providing support to hold your blooms in place.

Think carefully about the colour and any pattern of your potential vase. Remember it is

Invaluable tips

❀ Try to keep the height of your cutting material in proportion to the vase you have chosen. The arrangement should be as tall again as the vase. If your flowers are too tall they will appear top-heavy; if too small they will look dumpy.

❀ If you are using foliage and fillers, place these in your vase first to create some structure and then fill in with your flowers.

❀ Using odd numbers, say three or five stems, of a particular flower works well. Odd numbers are much more pleasing to the eye and will make the arrangement look balanced.

❀ With cottage-garden-type flowers and simple arrangements, it can be very effective to try to recreate the feeling of them growing in a garden. One way to do this is by grouping a few stems of the same flower together, rather than dotting single blooms through the arrangement.

❀ Trim your flowers, filler and foliage stems to different heights. There should be shorter stems towards the edge of your vase with stems gradually getting taller towards the middle. Again this is trying to replicate how the flowers would be growing naturally. It also allows the different blooms to be seen and appreciated.

❀ Think about where your flowers will be displayed. If it is up against a wall, only the front and sides will be seen, so arrange your flowers with this in mind. There is no point in putting lovely flowers around the back where nobody can see them, and anyway you will need tall flowers at the back of the vase. If the vase is to sit in the middle of a table it will be seen from all sides, so spread your flowers throughout the arrangement and have the tallest flowers in the middle of the vase, with the height of other blooms gradually decreasing. This means everyone will have a chance to see your beautiful flowers.

❀ Consider the size of your arrangement and where you plan to put it. A large dramatic display may seem like a good idea for a dining table, but I know from experience that your guests will just spend the night playing peek-a-boo. Eventually you will all get fed up with having to talk through plant material, and the vase will have to be moved somewhere else. Similarly, a bedside table is not the right spot for something too big and dominating, where it is likely to be knocked over; it is much better to opt for a small posy of scented flowers in such positions.

your flowers that are the stars of the show, and overly patterned vases will compete with your flowers for attention.

Some colours such as red may be harder to match with your flowers. If most of your flowers are going to be in pastel colours, it would be much better to build up a collection of vases that will work with them.

For flowers with much shorter stems, such as snowdrops, primroses and grape hyacinths, you will require much smaller vases. Look out

for old glass medicine bottles in pretty blues and greens, which work well.

Why not pop into your local charity shops or visit markets and antique shops to see what you can find. Vintage china, pewter jugs and even teapots all make great quirky vases. Pieces that may be unique, and that have not been mass produced, will give a much more individual touch, and it is possible to pick up some real bargains. Check to make sure there are no cracks, and if you are worried ask if you

Many florists swear by oasis. This foam-like material can be used in all sorts of containers to provide support for flowers. You soak the oasis and then push the flowers' stems into it. I live in an oasis-free zone though. Oasis is not a reusable or recyclable material and is an added expense. Arranging flowers in an oasis takes a lot more time too.

If you want to use a tea cup or other container as a vase, but it will not provide enough support for your flowers, there are alternatives to oasis.

- You can create a grid across the top of the vase using adhesive tape. Leave small holes into which you insert the plant stems.
- You can buy flower frogs. These are mounds with stem-sized holes in them, and they are available in plastic, metal, glass or ceramic. Place them on the bottom of a container such as a wide bowl.
- Chicken wire scrunched up in the bottom of your container is a useful alternative to oasis, but be careful it does not scratch any vintage china or glass vessel.

can put some water in the vessel to check that your potential purchase is watertight. If it is not or you can actually see a crack but you still love it, all may not be lost. As long as you can get to the crack easily, and you will not see any repair, you could mend it with silicon sealant.

If you do fancy something new, why not seek out something made in recycled glass, which is much better for the environment. A recycled glass vase needs 40 per cent less energy in its manufacture than a new glass one.

Reusing glass jars and tin cans will not cost anything, and they can look very beautiful filled with a collection of flowers. And what could be greener than to arrange your home-grown cut flowers in recycled vases?

Caring for your vases

Keeping your vases clean is important. Apart from grimy vases looking unattractive, the build-up of bacteria will shorten the life of your flowers.

Hot soapy water is normally sufficient to clean a vase, but I can definitely recommend investing in an old-fashioned bottlebrush to clean all those hard-to-reach places inside your vases.

For really small glass vases and any with particularly narrow necks, you can buy tubs of tiny copper beads, which you can gently swill around, inside your vase, with a little water. The copper is soft enough not to scratch the glass. You can reuse the balls, but they do need to be dried thoroughly before storing, to prevent them corroding.

Why not grow a collection of grasses, seed heads and flowers such as these in your cutting patch?

This blue and white collection sums up spring for me. It contains grape hyacinth, *Primula sieboldii* 'Snowflake', forget-me-nots, *Primula denticulata* var. *alba* and ivory *Anemone coronaria*.

RIGHT Small delicate flowers such as grape hyacinths (*Muscari*) are hard to buy as cut flowers but easy to grow yourself for picking.

BELOW *Anemone coronaria* are versatile flowers that work well on their own or in mixed arrangements.

Simple arrangements are often the most pleasing. Small bottles and jars make perfect receptacles.

OPPOSITE *Tulipa* 'Verona', *T.* 'Purissima', *Erysimum cheiri* 'Ivory White', white honesty and a few stems of newly emerging leaves here create an eye-catching arrangement.

LEFT *Narcissus* 'Actaea' is an early-flowering *Poeticus* variety that appears in mid-spring.

RIGHT This wallflower, *Erysimum cheiri* 'Ivory White', captures the freshness of spring.

OPPOSITE Scented stocks and honesty look marvellous when arranged with tulips and some foraged branches of hawthorn (*Crataegus monogyna*).

ABOVE A simple jumble of flowers can look so pretty and is easy to create.

RIGHT The rich colours of *Anemone coronaria* look stunning when arranged simply on their own.

LEFT *Dianthus barbatus* 'Green Trick' vies for attention amid *Scabiosa atropurpurea* 'Black Cat', drumstick alliums, white *Daucus carota*, *Centaurea cyanus* 'Black Ball' and pink statice.

The grasses *Agrostis nebulosa* and greater quaking grass combine with the double-flowered feverfew to introduce a natural feel to this lovely arrangement.

OPPOSITE
Early summer
brings the first
pickings of
sweet Williams
and lady's
mantle.

ABOVE Seek out beautiful
handmade vases like this one
from Tara Davidson, a ceramicist
from Gloucestershire, UK.

LEFT The vibrant orange of these
Iceland poppies contrasts well with
the blue-green of the old glass
bottles in which they are placed.

LEFT A mix of blue cornflowers, feverfew, yellow statice and *Achillea* 'Terracotta' is here combined with *Dianthus barbatus* 'Green Trick' and a few poppy seed heads.

BELOW I love how the pink-tinged squirrel tail grass catches the light, along with white sweet rocket, triteleia and *Allium caeruleum*.

OPPOSITE Sunflowers can often be hard to combine in arrangements because of the size of the flowers. The small blooms of *Helianthus debilis* 'Vanilla Ice' are easier to use than larger ones and are mixed here with *Ammi majus*, snapdragons, statice, white scabious and panicum.

RIGHT Pickings of apple mint
and Bowles's mint give a lovely
fragrance to vases and are mixed
here with lady's mantle, statice
and floss flower.

BELOW Collect jars and tins from
the kitchen for pretty containers
for your posies. They are perfect
for showing off the tiny details of
grasses and flowers such as blue
lace flower.

OPPOSITE I love the
tall spires of larkspur
arranged simply in
glass bottles.

OPPOSITE The rich colours of *Daucus carota* 'Black Knight', Peruvian lily (*Alstroemeria*) and chrysanthemums contrast with a second flush of flowers from lady's mantle.

ABOVE These hot colours of early autumn comprise *Helenium* combined with *Rudbeckia hirta* 'Prairie Sun', *Crocosmia* 'Lucifer' and *Deschampsia cespitosa* 'Goldtau'.

RIGHT A hedgerow harvest of brambles, hip and haws is eye-catching in a simple white jug.

Rich
pickings

Supplementing
your patch

The idea behind a dedicated cut flower patch is to grow highly productive flowers somewhere you can ruthlessly pick them, snipping away and not worrying about leaving bare patches. Viewing these flowers as a crop will mean you do not feel guilty about harvesting them.

Although your cut flower patch is the place to grow high-yielding annuals and biennials, you do not need to restrict yourself to these plants in your vases. There are herbaceous perennials, shrubs and even trees that can provide you with extra cutting material. They are not plants to decimate with your snips, but they will provide you with perhaps four or five stems here and there, to add to your arrangements. They might be plants you already grow but have never thought about cutting for the house. Perhaps you have a section of your garden you want to redesign, or you have moved to a new house and have a blank gardening canvas staring back at you. By including plants that look great and that will also provide you with extra cutting material for your vases, you will be making your garden work more effectively.

If you choose your plants carefully, even in a small garden, you can build up a good selection of plants that will boost your cut flower patch or make pretty displays in their own right. Some plants produce stunning seed heads,

Combine an autumnal walk with a spot of foraging.

which can be harvested for use indoors. These might be annuals, which can be grown on your cutting patch, or perennials, which could be planted in your borders.

It is not just your garden that can provide you with extra pickings. In autumn, winter and early spring, when cutting material is scarce, why not try a spot of foraging from the hedgerows? There is no better way of bringing a touch of seasonality into your home than to pick a few sprigs of wild rose with hips or pussy willow (*Salix*).

In the garden

The key to choosing and growing plants for extra pickings is to use your imagination. Sometimes the flowers produced might not be big or showy – and certainly not the sort of flowers you would see in a bought arrangement – but that does not mean they do not have value as cutting material.

In the 1930s, Constance Spry revolutionised the art of flower arranging and ideas of what could be used. Before her time, floristry was still about large blowsy arrangements, and the style had not moved on from the Victorian and Edwardian periods. Her ideas were radical for the time, and in many ways still seem so, as she used lichen-covered stems or branches of larch (*Larix*) covered with cones and even found inspiration from the vegetable patch by including cabbage leaves in her arrangements.

Picking through
the seasons

Gems in your garden

If you are lucky enough to have a garden it may contain a wide range of plants that you can use to supplement those from your cutting patch.

Winter

You would think late autumn and winter might be a barren time for picking plant material for a vase, but it need not be. Winter-flowering shrubs tend to produce small flowers, which can be invaluable in arrangements. It is a waste of energy for such shrubs to produce large flowers at a time of year when these are most likely to be damaged by the bad weather. Instead winter-flowering shrubs have evolved so they produce incredibly perfumed flowers and, if it was not for this, their small blooms would otherwise go unnoticed. It is quite strange really that some of the most strongly perfumed flowers bloom in winter, but with fewer pollinating insects around they need to try much harder to attract them.

A couple of stems of these winter-flowering shrubs, picked and brought into your home, are a real delight. In the warmth, the flowers will unfurl from their tight buds. Up close, perhaps on your desk or a kitchen windowsill, you can appreciate the beauty of these flowers. You may not want to linger outdoors in midwinter, but when warm and cosy inside the house you can study these flowers at close quarters. Maybe it is because there is so little else of cheer during the short cold days of winter that I love these plants so much.

There are few joys as great as the heady scent of *Viburnum × bodnantense* 'Dawn' filling my kitchen. Its dark stems and white flowers with a hint of candy-floss pink look lovely arranged in glass bottles and have an oriental feel about them. They will happily last ten

Although the flowers may be tiny, the scent of winter-flowering honeysuckle is incredible.

The sweetly scented flowers of *Viburnum* × *bodnantense* 'Dawn' brighten up any winter's day.

days like this – even more they are if kept somewhere cool, although the perfume will not then be as powerful after such a long time.

The winter-flowering honeysuckles, *Lonicera* × *purpusii* and *L. fragrantissima*, form woody shrubs, unlike their summer-flowering climbing relatives. They do not have much to endear them for nine months of the year, with their nondescript foliage and slightly unkempt appearance, but when you smell their tiny white flowers in winter it is impossible not to want one in your garden. A few stems arranged in a tall vase make an elegant display for a dining table, and depending on the weather you may well have a few stems to pick for Christmas. In my own garden they start flowering from late autumn and will continue sporadically through to early spring.

Wintersweet (*Chimonanthus praecox*) is a plant I came across fairly recently, and have not as yet got round to planting in my garden, but it is top of my wish list. *Chimonanthus*, which means 'winter flower' in Greek, is not a commonly grown shrub, perhaps because it has a reputation for taking up to seven years from planting to flowering. The first time I came across it was on a cold frosty day in late winter. Once I had smelled its sweetly spiced flowers I had to go back several times to have another sniff. The flowers are small and quite unusual. They hang down from bare stems, looking a little like a shaggy bonnet, and are a buttery yellow with a waxy look to the outer petals. As these open they reveal an inner circle of reddish purple petals. Just like the other winter-flowering shrubs I have mentioned, wintersweet looks unremarkable at other times of the year, but it is easy to forget that in the depths of winter when it produces such beautifully fragrant flowers.

With all three of these plants you can pick stems when they are just coming into bud, and then over the coming days you can appreciate the blooms as they gradually open.

The autumn-flowering cherry *Prunus* × *subhirtella* 'Autumnalis' has a subtle scent of almonds. Its flowers, which appear from late autumn through to early spring, are spectacularly pretty. With their white petals with a blush of pink, the blossoms look more delicate than those of spring-flowering cherries. However this autumn-flowering cherry will stop blooming if the weather turns particularly cold. A few stems of it look beautiful indoors, especially in midwinter, when the Christmas decorations have come down and the house looks a little bare. It also produces attractively coloured foliage in spring and autumn, so is a good, year-round tree for a gardener looking for extra cutting material. Autumn-flowering cherry can become quite a substantial tree, so is not suitable for a very small garden.

Corkscrew hazel (*Corylus avellana* 'Contorta') was discovered growing in the wild by the Victorian gardener Canon Ellacombe of Bitten, Gloucestershire, UK. Its contorted stems caught his attention one day, and he decided to propagate from the plant and gave the offspring to his gardening friend E.A. Bowles. It is now available to all gardeners. Its stems make a useful addition in a vase and look attractive enough to be used on their own, particularly if picked in mid- and late winter when its catkins open into attractive yellow droplets, dangling down from the stems and contrasting dramatically against the dark silhouettes of the twisted twigs. The downside is that corkscrew hazel can look a tad scruffy when in leaf, so it is best not to give it too prominent a position in the garden.

Spring

Although the days may be getting longer and there is warmth returning to the sun, the spring months can be a frustrating time for flower picking. There is an eagerness to get out into the garden and get growing again, but often the weather has other ideas.

Bulbs and some of the winter-flowering shrubs mentioned earlier will provide some of your first cut flowers of the year. My favourite plants in spring capture the zing, vibrancy and freshness of new growth, and it is this feeling I want to create in my vases.

Forsythia is one of the first shrubs to flower in spring, producing its yellow flowers on bare stems. This shot of colour is just what is needed after the greyness of winter. Forsythia has

fallen out of favour with many. Its season of interest is admittedly short, but if you pick a few stems when you see the flower buds forming and bring them indoors they will last a couple of weeks, gradually opening and revealing their vibrantly coloured petals.

Spring is synonymous with blossom. A few branches in a vase look perfect on their own. The flowers often signify a fruitful bounty later in the year, but whether you want to sacrifice some of your crop is up to you. I have a crab apple (*Malus*) in my garden, and picking a few stems, particularly if the blossom coincides with Easter, is a special treat.

The acid-green, pom-pom flowers of guelder rose (*Viburnum opulus*) look stunning in arrangements. As the flowers age, the green

The bright yellow colour of forsythia flowers is a welcome sight in early spring.

fades to cream and then white, hence its other common name – snowball bush. It flowers from mid-spring to early summer, and is great when combined with richly coloured tulips.

Primroses (*Primula vulgaris*) are one of my favourite flowers and one of my best cut flower discoveries. The palest of yellow petals look so delicate, but they are surprisingly tough little plants. They are native to woodlands and hedgerows in the UK and parts of northern Europe and will establish quickly in most gardens. Not only will you be able to divide plants after several years, to increase numbers, but you will also find self-sown plants appearing all over your garden. Primroses used to be a popular cut flower. From the late-nineteenth to mid-twentieth centuries the flowers were picked in vast numbers from the hedgerows and woods, delicately packed and sent to flower markets. This was an important source of income for flower growers and became known as 'primrose money'. Few people however consider picking them nowadays, but for me primroses are one of the simplest and most beautiful of cut flowers. Their stems are quite small in comparison to other flowers, so you will need some tiny vases. A few stems arranged in a small glass

medicine bottle looks so pretty, and the flowers last an incredible ten days once picked. Primroses bloom over a long period too. In my own garden I will often have them in flower at Christmas, and they will continue right through until mid-spring. There is no need to pick primroses from the wild as they grow easily in a garden setting, and once established they produce masses of flowers so you do not need to feel guilty about picking them.

Primroses are not the only members of the primula family that make great cut flowers. There is a huge selection to choose from. Why not try the Gold-laced Group hybrids?

With their taller, more robust stems they make unusual flowers for a small posy. Or what about P. *sieboldii*, with its elegant flowers delicately cut like snowflakes? For more vibrant colours and taller stems grow varieties of P. *japonica* or P. *beesiana*. In fact the choice is so great that growing primulas as cut flowers could become quite addictive. Primulas prefer shady conditions and moist soils, so are perfect for sneaking in a patch of cut flowers where other plants will not grow. You could even edge a shady path at the allotment with them since they take up little space, forming neat hummocks of leaves.

Summer

Summer is the time for herbaceous perennials. Your cut flower patch will by now be at its peak, and you should be able to pick at least two buckets a week of flowers from it. However it is still nice to be able to pick the occasional bloom from your garden borders.

One of the best plants to grow for this time of year is Hattie's pincushion (*Astrantia*), an easy-going plant that can cope with most soils and conditions; it has the additional benefit of being a long-lasting cut flower. It is certainly a flower worthy of closer inspection. What look like petals are in fact bracts, papery in texture and often beautifully marked; with the light behind them, they look like stained glass. The centre of the bracts is made up of tiny multiple flowers held on stalks, which explain the plant's common name. Hattie's pincushion is one of the longest-flowering herbaceous perennials, with its first flowers appearing in late spring and the plants still blooming in mid-autumn. Colours range from pinks and crimsons to greenish white. I particularly like *A. major* 'Ruby Wedding' and *A. major* var. *rosea*. The white varieties prefer a little shade, but the reds and pinks need more sunshine for the true depth of their colours to shine through.

I love to include this plant in arrangements. Just a couple of stems gives a natural relaxed hedgerow feel to a bunch of flowers.

Yarrow (*Achillea*) is another plant that blooms over a long period. Small flowers are held in densely packed clusters on top of tall stems, and they are magnets for hoverflies and butterflies. The varieties we grow in the garden are closely related to *A millefolium*, which you may see growing on grassy verges. By including cultivated versions of wild-growing plants you can give arrangements a naturalistic feel, which I love. It is suggested in the *Iliad* that the wounds of the Greek warrior Achilles were

OPPOSITE Hattie's pincushion grows wild in parts of the Balkans at the edge of woodland glades. Their wild and natural look means they are perfect for creating a countryside feel to floral arrangements.

ABOVE LEFT Yarrow is an easy-to-grow perennial, and it makes a good cut flower.

ABOVE RIGHT Pink-flowered Peruvian lily (*Alstroemeria*) goes well with the green flower buds of scabious, my favourite 'filler' *Daucus carota* 'Black Knight' and sumptuous chrysanthemums picked from my cut flower garden.

Sow feverfew under cover in late summer, so you have plants that will flower the following year.

The flowers last incredibly well at up to two weeks. The one downside is that the plants are only frost-hardy. They can cope with light frosts, but anything below $-5°C/23°F$ will kill them. In some areas it may be possible to get Peruvian lily through winter by mulching the plant heavily in autumn with a thick layer of compost, bracken or composted bark, to protect its tuberous root system. In areas where the cold may last a long time it is advisable to lift the plants in autumn, put into pots of compost and store them over winter somewhere frost-free. You can then replant in spring. Peruvian lilies produce a mass of flowers, but these need careful harvesting. If you follow my advice (page 142) for pulling the flower stems from the base of the plant rather than cutting them, your Peruvian lilies will be incredibly productive.

If you want a classic cottage garden feel to your arrangements, growing a few feverfew (*Tanacetum parthenium*) plants is a must. This is a short-lived perennial that grows easily from seed and can be treated as a hardy annual. I sow mine in late summer since the plants then produce flowers much earlier and more prolifically than from spring-sown seeds. Being more commonly grown in herb gardens, feverfew is often thought to have derived its name from its ability to reduce fevers, but the name may be a corruption of 'featherfew', relating to the feathered form of the leaves. Feverfew has been used in herbal medicine for thousands of years and is now believed to hold properties that can alleviate the symptoms of migraines. Originally from south-east Europe

treated with this plant – hence its botanical name. Generally yarrow is bought as a plant, but it is possible to grow it from seed, and from an early sowing indoors in late winter it will flower about four months later. Try Summer Pastels Group or Summer Berries Group.

The Peruvian lily (*Alstroemeria*) sounds pretty exotic and has a more tropical feel to it than the other flowers I have suggested. Originally found growing in South America, its vibrantly coloured flowers, with spotted and feathered patterns, look unusual. Despite this, the flowers work well when mixed with more traditional-style blooms. They certainly do not look out of place on a cutting patch.

A bucket of joy – home-grown cut flowers make the work earlier in the year worthwhile.

Rosa A Shropshire Lad is a classic beauty with a delicate scent.

and the Caucasus, feverfew has aromatic leaves and pretty, daisy-like flowers with rings of white petals and yellow centres. My favourite is the double-flowered form *Tanacetum parthenium* 'Flore Pleno', although it is strangely hard to come by. All feverfew tend to self-sow, although this will be less of a problem if you pick the flowers. It is still worth letting a few flowers go to seed, which you can collect and sow in summer for more plants. After the first flush of blooms cut the whole plant back down to the ground and give a feed of liquid seaweed fertiliser. You should get a second crop of flowering stems.

Helen's flower (*Helenium*) is a brilliant addition to any garden, but for the cut flower lover it is a special plant. It is as cut-and-come-again as you will get with a perennial, so you do not have to worry that picking will mean fewer blooms for the garden. Helen's flower lasts well once cut and, if you choose your variety carefully, it will produce flowers over a long period. *Helenium* 'Sahin's Early Flowerer' is one of the best and is true to its name, flowering in early summer – a good month before other varieties start to bloom – and it will still be producing flowers into mid-autumn. With their chocolate-brown centres surrounded by a ring of orange petals tinged yellow, they are especially cheerful flowers and are perfect arranged with grasses and black-eyed Susans. Helen's flower is poisonous and contact with the skin can cause irritation, so always wear gloves when picking them.

Where would summer be without roses? There is nothing that captures summer quite as well as a rose. I love them, despite the thorns and their tendency to suffer from pests and diseases. But the roses I love bare little resemblance to the imported varieties that can

The simple beauty of mock orange flowers mean they deserve to take centre stage. Therefore cut a few stems and arrange them on their own.

be bought all year round. These commercially grown roses lack a delicacy that garden-grown ones possess, and there is something about their uniformity that gives them an artificial feel. They do not have the blowsiness that I think is an essential characteristic of a true rose, and most importantly they lack any perfume. Give someone a bunch of roses, and the first thing they do is hold it to their face to drink in the heady scent they expect to be there. Then watch their reaction as they, disappointingly, discover there is no scent to speak of. It is such an instinctive reaction, and yet scented roses are rare as cut flowers. The reason for this is that fragrant roses have the shortest lifespan once cut, making them unsuitable for commercial growing. Stem length, the size of the flower head, productivity and transport life are what matter to commercial growers. The result unfortunately and ironically is flowers that lack any real beauty. I would much rather pick a scented rose from my garden, which might last only a few days but has all the attributes I want. I grow *Rosa* A Shropshire Lad, *R*. Gertrude Jekyll and *R*. Geoff Hamilton, and while I do not often pick them when I do it is a real pleasure.

Mock orange (*Philadelphus*) is one of my earliest plant-related memories. There was one growing by the garden gate of the home I grew up in. I loved that plant and its beautiful ivory flowers, but it was its intoxicating scent that was most beguiling, reminiscent of orange blossom, hence its common name of mock orange. For most of the year mock orange is not the most inspiring plant, and in a small space it really should work harder for its place, but sometimes your heart has to rule your head. Mock orange flowers from the beginning of early summer for about six weeks. I love to pick

a few stems and put them in a vase. They are plants that are happy in a variety of conditions and establish quickly, so, within a few years of planting, your shrub should be substantial enough to allow you to cut a few stems.

Autumn

Your cut flowers will have passed their peak as autumn takes hold. However in the garden there are plants that are coming into their own and are perfect when arranged with the late-flowering annuals and dahlias from your cutting patch.

Stonecrop (*Sedum*) is a must-have addition to any garden. It can cope with drought or incessant rain, is loved by bees, hoverflies and butterflies and gives a long season of interest. And if that was not enough it makes a great cut flower. Stonecrop is not cut-and-come-again, but it forms large clumps fairly readily. The glaucous green stems and flower buds, which appear from midsummer, look lovely picked and used in arrangements, but I prefer to wait until late summer or autumn for the flat heads of tiny flowers. Once cut they can last up to two weeks. If other blooms in the vase have died, remove the stonecrop, trim the stems and reuse with fresh flowers. Varieties of S. *spectabile* are some of the best for picking; try white-flowered S. *spectabile* 'Stardust' or dark pink S. 'Herbstfreude'.

A native of South Africa, montbretia (*Crocosmia*) grows from corms that look like hairy squished bulbs. This member of the iris family forms clumps of strap-like leaves and flowers from midsummer until mid-autumn. It sends out exotic-looking, funnel-shaped blooms in hot colours ranging from yellow through orange to almost red. For optimum

Whether freshly cut or dried, the delicate flower heads of the grass *Agrostis nebulosa* work well in a vase.

length of time with it looking good in a vase, pick the stems when the first flowers (at the bottom) have just opened. The others will continue to develop all the way up the stem. You can also pick the stems when they have gone to seed (see page 197).

It is difficult to produce foliage, particularly evergreen foliage, for cutting when you have only a small space at your disposal. One plant I can recommend though, which comes into its own in autumn, is *Viburnum tinus* 'Gwenllian'. Although it is evergreen and so possible to pick from at any time, I prefer to wait until autumn when flowers appear on its stems. Clusters of tiny crimson buds open into star-like, white flowers, which are blushed pink. When combined with the evergreen foliage, they look great arranged with the scabious, ammi and wild carrot from your cut flower patch. Viburnum can be a little slow to get going, but once it does it will form a bushy shrub 1.5–2.5m/5–8ft tall and the same spread, providing you with a good source of evergreen cuttings.

Grasses

These have been a fairly recent discovery for me, in terms of picking and bringing indoors. I had simply never considered them, but then one day I had picked some autumnal flowers – asters, black-eyed Susan and Helen's flower – and wanted something foliage-like that reflected the season. The golden seed heads of *Deschampsia cespitosa* 'Goldtau', the colour of a swaying cornfield, growing in one of my raised beds caught my eye, so I thought I would give them a try. To my delight they looked great, and they also lasted and lasted. Not only did they work when arranged in a vase with other flowers, but they also looked great in their dried form with other seed heads.

Pheasant's tail grass (*Anemanthele lessoniana*) is another perennial grass I like to use, and I include some annual grasses on the cut flower patch and dotted about my garden. The hardy annual greater quaking grass (see pages 106–7) can be used fresh or dry, as can *Panicum elegans* 'Frosted Explosion' and *Agrostis nebulosa*.

If you have already got grasses in your garden, experiment to see which ones work. I have even seen a stunning arrangement using the huge seed heads of giant feather grass (*Stipa gigantea*).

Among this hand-tied mix of seed heads and grasses are to be found teasel, honesty, love-in-a-mist, poppies and the orange seed pods of montbretia.

Seed heads

Even the words 'dried floral arrangement' sound old-fashioned, fusty and dusty and represent the complete antithesis of the vibrancy and freshness of your home-grown cut flowers. However I have been won over by them – well, some of them at least.

In late autumn and winter, when the cut flower patch is no longer producing, a few seed heads collected from the allotment and garden provide some welcome decoration. I think the key to dried plants is not to hold on to them for too long. I tend to get rid of mine in mid-winter. At this point I am craving for some vibrancy to lift my spirits and will look to buy early local daffodils to fill the gap until my own bulbs appear. Until then though, golden grasses, the silvery blue opium poppy heads and the papery, moon-like discs of honesty are a beautiful celebration of the dying embers of the cutting patch and garden.

There are some plants worth growing for their seed heads alone. I love opium poppy flowers, but their ethereal blooms do not last for long once cut. However their seed pods are stunningly beautiful in their own right. Their swollen, blue, round pods with unusual frilled tops develop a silvery white bloom as they dry. I use the seed pods fresh in arrangements throughout the summer and autumn. Their cool blue colour works especially well with pastel colours, but I also like to pick some seed heads for drying. It is best to pick opium poppy pods when they are plump and the seeds inside are still immature. A mature seed head will rattle. Inside a poppy pod are hundreds, if not thousands, of tiny black seeds. Place your poppy stems upside down into a paper bag so that the seed heads are inside, secure the top with a rubber band or some twine and hang somewhere dry and warm. An airing cupboard is ideal but a shed would work. The real key is to not expose the seed heads to moisture because it will encourage mould. As they dry inside the bag the heads will gradually open and release seeds into the bag. It should take 2–3 weeks in an airing cupboard for the seed heads to fully dry – longer if left somewhere cooler. Shake the seed heads well, inside the bag, to release any remaining seeds then carefully remove the heads from the bag, leaving the seeds inside. You can use the seed heads straightaway or store them somewhere dust-free. Move the seeds to paper envelopes, label and store them until next spring, when you can sow again.

Love-in-a-mist produces eye-catching seed pods. Just like poppies, you can use them fresh – straight from the plant – or dried. Pick and treat as you would for poppies.

Honesty produces pretty, white and pink flowers in early summer, but it is really for the seed pods that you should grow it. The silvery papery discs are particularly delicate. To protect the seed pods, which can be easily damaged by the weather, it is best to pick them when the outer discs have dried but are still intact. Carefully remove the outer discs yourself as well as the fat dark seeds inside; you will then be left with branching stems of shimmering seed pods.

The papery globular seed heads of *Scabiosa stellata* 'Ping Pong' are stunning. Their structure is fascinating, being divided into different sections in which each seed is held. The flowers are pretty too and can be cut, although I prefer to grow this variety purely for its seed heads, using other varieties of scabious to provide cut flowers. Allow these to dry on the plant before picking.

The intriguing seed heads of opium poppies (left), the
balloon-like seed pods of love-in-a-mist (centre) and the
silvery seed pods of honesty (right) all catch the light.

Montbretias produce attractive-looking
seed pods held on tall stems, which make an
unusual addition to your dried material. Pick
when the seed pods are green and use fresh in
arrangements or wait until they have turned
orange and started to become wizened. Pick
and strip away any foliage and then tie a small
bunch together and hang somewhere warm
and dry. To retain their colour it is best to dry
montbretia somewhere out of direct sunlight.
The seed heads should take 2–3 weeks to dry.

The faded flower heads of sevenbark
(*Hydrangea arborescens*) in my garden are one
of my favourite decorations for the autumn

and winter house. I allow them to fade on the
plant, and then I pick them from late autumn
onwards. They look beautiful on the plant
when covered in frost, and I also love them in
vases in the house – their silhouettes cast on
the walls by the fading winter sun.

Foraging

Searching for food has become popular in recent
years. Once it was a necessity to supplement
meagre food supplies, and we are now
gradually rediscovering our connection with
the countryside. So why not extend the idea of
foraging for food to searching for plant material

Berries and branches picked from the hedgerows look good in an autumnal arrangement.

to decorate the house? My foraging season begins in early autumn with a few branches covered in acorns, and ends in early spring with some stems of blackthorn (*Prunus spinosa*). There are a few rules to observe (see page 200).

What to forage?

Autumn is a period of fruitfulness in the hedgerows. Rosehips, hawthorn (*Crataegus monogyna*) berries and even stems of blackberries (*Rubus fruticosus*) will last 10–14 days in water and bring a touch of the countryside indoors. Some plants have vicious thorns, but these can easily be removed with a pair of secateurs or flower snips.

Branches with acorns and sweet chestnuts (*Castanea sativa*) look good in a vase, but you need to pick these earlier than you might imagine as they will have dropped from the tree by mid-autumn. The vibrant green spiky seed pods of the sweet chestnut make unusual and attractive additions to an autumnal arrangement when combined with the rich colours of autumnal flowers such as dahlias.

The spiky, hedgehog-like seed heads of teasels (*Dipsacus fullonum*) can be found dotted about the countryside from early autumn onwards. They can get damaged by the weather, so pick them early in autumn and put them somewhere dry, like a shed. After a couple of weeks shake the seeds into a tray or bucket and you can either get rid of these seeds or use them to grow your own teasels. Teasels come with some vicious thorns. To rub them away run the blade of your snips gently up and down each stem.

A few sprigs of crab apples look unusual and give you the chance to appreciate the beautiful colours and patterns of these miniature apples up close. Arrange them with some berries and a few bits of evergreen from your garden to bring a flavour of the hedgerow into your home.

Spiky holly (*Ilex*) and ivy (*Hedera*), with their long stems and lax habits, make great additions to a garland, which you can use to adorn the top of a bookcase or mirror. They will become dry and shrivelled over time but if picked a few days before Christmas will survive the holiday period.

A few stems of larch (*Larix*) can make a striking display. By winter its deciduous needles will have dropped to reveal the small and

The architectural
seed heads of teasels
and sevenbark give
long-lasting pleasure.

Foraging rules

- Never pick from gardens even if it is a hedgerow boundary.
- Always ask the landowner's permission and never trespass.
- Do not take from land that is part of a nature reserve or protected in any way.
- Some plants are protected by law and should never be picked. Ensure you are well informed as to which these are.
- Do not strip a plant bare. A couple of stems here and there is fine and will go unnoticed, but should you take any more you will deprive others of the enjoyment of them, as well as take away a source of potential food for wildlife.
- Never uproot a plant.
- Picking from plants that are in abundance is best. Blackthorn and rosehips are common and can survive some foraging.
- Wild flowers are a rare enough sight and should be left to prosper in the countryside. You should not need to pick flowers anyway now that you have your own blossoming cut flower patch.
- Pick plants you recognise. It is easy to confuse some plants. Cow parsley (*Anthriscus sylvestris*) and hemlock (*Conium maculatum*), for example, have similar white umbelliferous flowers. Cow parsley is safe to pick, while hemlock most definitely is not. If in doubt, do not pick.
- Wear gloves when picking and arranging, as some plants have thorns and prickles and others may exude poisonous sap, which could cause skin irritations.

This attractive grouping of blackberries, rowan berries and larch stems is truly inspirational.

beautifully formed pine cones dotted along the branches. The dark stems and cones create a lovely silhouette when arranged on their own.

Take a walk after a spell of windy weather and there will often be branches blown from trees on the ground. Windfalls can also snap off some gorgeous, lichen-covered branches. Arrange them with some of the seed heads you have collected or put them on their own in a tall glass vase filled with pine cones to cover the stems. Hang some small glass decorations on them and you have the perfect decoration for the Christmas table.

The incredibly soft buds of pussy willow and stems of hazel slowly unfurling their sulphurous yellow catkins herald the arrival of spring. After a long dark winter they bring with them much hope of the growing season to come. Pick these stems at the bud stage so you can watch both slowly open in your home.

Blackthorn (*Prunus spinosa*) is a classic plant of the countryside and the last of my forage pickings before my cut flower patch starts to produce blooms for picking. It bears tiny, delicate white flowers in early spring, which cover the plant as if it has been dusted with snow. Its blossom is a welcome sight in late winter and early spring and I think it is exquisite in its simple beauty. A few blackthorn stems are all that is needed, and they last a week in water. Do not be fooled by the dainty flowers – vicious thorns run along each stem and give the plant its name. Fortunately they are easily removed with your snips.

Natural Christmas decorations are kinder to the environment. Put them on the compost heap when the festivities are over.

The dried flower heads of sevenbark make stunning silhouettes in autumn and winter light.

Traditional
flower growing

A rich history

There are times when even if you are self-sufficient in flowers you will want to buy some for a big event or send some to friends or family. This does not mean that you have to resort to purchasing imported flowers. There may well be an increasing number of excellent artisan flower growers in your locality.

There was a time when many countries supplied all their own cut flower needs. The perishable nature of the flowers meant that

Early twentieth-century daffodil pickers on the Isles of Scilly. These islands are located off the tip of Cornwall, in the UK, where there is a rich heritage of flower growing.

it was only with the advent of air travel and motorway networks in the twentieth century that cheaper imported flowers made their way into such areas in mass-produced numbers.

Previously, in the nineteenth century, flower growing had been an important aspect of market gardening. The birth of railway transport meant that flowers picked one day could be transported quickly and easily to the local flower markets in major cities for sale the following day. Initially seen as a way of supplementing an income from fruit growing, flower production and particularly daffodil growing soon became a lucrative business in its own right. By the early 1900s, for example, Cornwall, in the UK, had become synonymous with daffodils. The south-facing slopes of the Tamar estuary, on the Cornwall and Devon border, were the perfect place to grow early-flowering crops. With the slopes of the valley sheltered from the prevailing winds and the mild winters, the ground warmed up early in spring. *Narcissus* 'Tamar Double White' was especially prized with its large, heavily scented blooms.

As demand for flowers grew, so too did the varieties grown. Violets (*Viola odorata*), lily-of-the-valley (*Convallaria majalis*), pinks (*Dianthus*), asters and anemones transformed fields into colourful patchworks. Flower growing reached its peak in the UK in the 1950s with more land devoted to flowers than fruit crops. Buildings made out of wood with corrugated iron roofs dotted the landscape. These packing houses were the hubs of the flower farms, with flowers being conditioned and packed ready for transport.

Ironically the railways, which were the reason for the indigenous flower-growing boom in the first place, were to be its downfall too in some countries. Cuts to the railway infrastructure, combined with increased use of road and air transport, resulted in flower imports growing to such an extent that it is estimated that in, for example, Britain they accounted for 80–90 per cent of cut flower sales by the end of the twentieth century.

However that tide may now have turned, with a resurgence in flower farming in recent years – and not just in the traditional flower-growing regions. In new areas there are also flower growers who care about seasonality and garden with the environment in mind. Their passion for flowers, and the hard work they put into cultivating them, is inspiring. By buying direct from these growers you get freshly cut, seasonal flowers which have a low environmental impact, and the growers will see the full reward for their efforts.

Growing your own cut flowers makes you appreciate the difference between fresh seasonal flowers and imported blooms. Once you have grown your own you will not want to resort to their bland imported cousins, and you do not need to. There is an excellent website (www.flowersfromthefarm.co.uk) which is for a network set up to support and promote British flower growers, allowing you to search for flower farmers across the country. It is well worth sourcing flower growers in your locality too and supporting them.

Green and Gorgeous are based in south Oxfordshire, UK and sell directly at farmers' markets. They also do weddings and have 'pick your own' Saturdays at their farm. www.greenandgorgeousflowers.co.uk/

Sara Willman grows a great range of beautiful seasonal cut flowers supplying clients in the Wiltshire area of England. @myflowerpatch

Common Farm Flowers can be found in Somerset, UK. The inspirational owner creates stunning arrangements and delivers all across the country. www.commonfarmflowers.com/

Organic Blooms, just outside Bristol, UK, is a truly wonderful place giving people with learning difficulties and mental health problems the opportunity to learn in a supportive environment. They deliver and you can also visit the site. If you do not believe in the power of plants to heal and teach then visit them and you will be blown away. www.organicblooms.co.uk/

The Wiggly Florist is one of the larger, British-only flower sellers. They grow their own and also buy in from other local growers. Their flowers conjure up the countryside at its best. www.wigglywigglers.co.uk/

Scented Narcissi will deliver beautifully scented daffodils grown by the flower farmers on the Isles of Scilly, UK, direct to your home. The mild, frost-free growing conditions on these islands off the tip of Cornwall mean there is no need to buy exotic imported flowers through the winter and into spring, when Scented Narcissi can supply you with daffodils instead. www.scentednarcissi.co.uk/

A year
on the patch

Through
the seasons

Spring on my cut flower patch

By early spring I am bursting with pent-up energy and the need to get growing again. I try to be patient and hold back, only planting those seeds I know can cope with the vagaries of the weather at this time of year. It is hard though not to go and sow everything on that first warm sunny day of the year, but I know I must resist.

Early spring is generally a month of preparation. There are the first weeds appearing, and it is essential to keep on top of them. I feed my biennials, which are slowly coming to life again, with seaweed meal to give them a boost. Going over the plants, and removing any yellowing, damaged and dead foliage, spruces them up and prevents any fungal diseases from establishing once the temperatures start to rise. It is a nice time of year because fellow gardeners start to appear again after the winter, and it is good to see activity on the allotments once more. There is a sense of anticipation about the growing season ahead.

The first flowers should be ready to pick by the end of the month. You would think I would be used to it by now, but I still get excited when I see the first flowers appearing. Stocks, with their heavily scented flowers, are one of my favourites. By mid-spring brown earth is starting to disappear, with tulips,

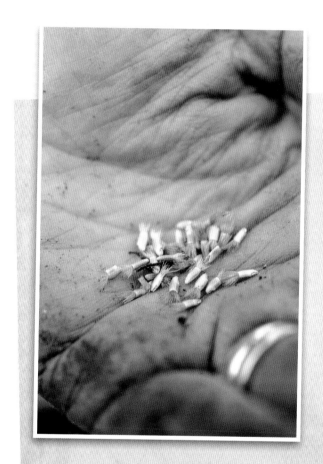

As winter comes to an end I cannot wait to get sowing again.

LEFT A few stems of delicate cherry blossom are a delight in spring.

The cool colours
of early spring
give way to the
vibrant ones
of tulips.

daffodils, stocks and wallflowers all flowering, and as late spring arrives the cutting patch is increasing production. Early mornings at this time of year are beautiful, the soft rays of sunshine giving everything a warm glow. The whole cutting patch feels fresh and full of life and there are not many better ways to start the day than to pick some honesty and tulips before breakfast. This early morning calm belies the fact that it is a frantic time in the gardening calendar, with plants to move on from windowsills and cold frames to the cut flower patch. There is also the worry that a late frost is never too far away.

Summer on my cut flower patch

By early summer I can breathe a sigh of relief since this year's flowers should all be in their final growing spaces now and my windowsills, cold frames and greenhouse have emptied. If I can, I will spend a few hours at the plot every other day, picking, deadheading, weeding and watering. None of this feels like a chore. In fact my cut flower patch is a place to which I escape – a calm and tranquil spot that soothes me and eases away the stresses of life. The youthfulness of spring has given way to a more relaxed feeling. Summer starts with pastel colours dominating the patch, but as the season progresses the colours become richer and deeper.

It is a strange time of year for me. It feels as if the gardening calendar has just started, and yet after the summer solstice we are moving towards winter again. If I allow myself time to dwell on this it can make me feel quite melancholic. Fortunately there is no time to mope as the cut flower patch is entering its peak of productivity.

Hardy annuals are flowering, the hazel wigwams are clothed in sweet peas and the plot is a riot of colour. I particularly love the mornings in mid- and late summer, when the sun rises early and there is a sense of the long, hot, lazy hazy day to come. The cut flower patch smells of summer – that heady mix of cut grass and scents from the flowers mingling in the warm still air. Butterflies silently flutter by as I pick my flowers, and bees are making the most of the nectar and pollen.

A hand-tied bouquet of flowers picked from my cutting patch makes an excellent gift for a friend.

Autumn on my cut flower patch

The jewel-like colours of the flowers on the cutting patch, combined with the lower light levels at this time of year, look stunning. There is still plenty to pick but I am also starting to look to the hedgerows for a few pieces to mix with my flowers, and planning any decorations for the house once I have to put the plot to bed for winter. Now is the time I go for walks, looking for teasels and lichen-covered branches. It is when I make notes of what has worked for me this season and what I might do differently next year.

Tidying up the cut flower patch makes me feel a little sad. While the enforced rest that winter brings is needed, the long dark nights are creeping ever closer, but for someone who loves being outdoors this is not a thrilling prospect. Still, planting out my biennials, which will flower next spring, fills me with renewed hope and excitement. I am thinking of new ideas, and the list of flowers for which I want to find space grows ever longer.

Then there is bulb planting. It is not my favourite gardening job, but when spring comes I am always glad I have done it. The changing light is noticeable now, and morning visits to the cutting patch require a jumper as there is a nip in the air. The scabious are still flowering, as are the half-hardy annuals such as coneflower (*Rudbeckia*) and zinnia, but it is the dahlias that are the real stars at this time of year.

Winter on my cut flower patch

Grey and brown are the colours of the plot now. Winters tend to be wet here, which makes me glad we put in the paths on the allotment. If we are lucky, and if there are any dry spells, I can still wander around without having to walk on the wet soil. The first frosts tend to arrive some time between late autumn and early winter, so now is the time for me to pull out the dying flowers, cut back perennials such as lady's mantle and dig up the dahlia tubers for storing over winter indoors.

I look at the cutting patch now, in the gloomy winter light, and it is hard to imagine that the desolate-looking site will be a riot of colour again. If we are lucky we will get some snow, which covers the plot like a fluffy duvet. Such a covering of snow turns the cutting patch into a winter wonderland, protecting plants below ground from the cold above. This shot of white breaks the monotony of the otherwise drab and dreary winter weather.

Then, as the snow melts, there are the first signs of new life, with the green spires of bulbs pushing through the surface of the soil, unperturbed by the cold above. There will be days when the sun shines and I can feel the warmth returning and there is a taste of spring, but the weather can change quickly and these days are fleeting.

It is a time for staying warm indoors, planning and organising for the new season on the cut flower patch. By late winter the first seeds can be sown. It is a good feeling to pop the hard, shot-like sweet pea seeds into their compost. And so the cycle begins again.

TOP Blackbirds often shelter from the cold wind in the trees surrounding my cutting patch.

ABOVE Frost lingering on leaves and other surfaces makes them sparkle in the low winter light.

Sowing and planting calendar

		Midwinter	Late winter	Early spring	Mid-spring	Late spring
Bulbs	Anemone coronaria			plant	plant	plant
	Daffodil (Narcissus)					
	Dahlia			plant	plant	
	Ornamental onions (Allium)					
	Triteleia laxa					
	Tulip (Tulipa)					
Seeds	Agrostis nebulosa			sow	sow	
	Ammi				sow	sow
	Black-eyed Susan (Rudbeckia hirta)			sow	sow	
	Blue lace flower (Trachymene coerulea)			sow	sow	
	Cornflower (Centaurea cyanus)			sow	sow	sow
	Cosmos				sow	sow
	Feverfew (Tanacetum parthenium)			sow		
	Floss flower (Ageratum houstonianum)		sow	sow		
	Greater quaking grass (Briza maxima)			sow	sow	
	Honesty (Lunaria annua)					
	Iceland poppy (Papaver nudicaule)					
	Larkspur (Consolida ajacis)			sow	sow	
	Love-in-a-mist (Nigella damascena)			sow	sow	sow
	Panicum elegans 'Frosted Explosion'		sow	sow		
	Scabiosa atropurpurea			sow	sow	
	Scabiosa stellata 'Ping Pong'			sow	sow	
	Snapdragon (Antirrhinum)		sow	sow	sow	
	Statice (Limonium sinuatum)		sow	sow		
	Stock (Matthiola)					
	Sunflower (Helianthus annuus)			sow	sow	
	Sweet pea (Lathyrus odoratus)		sow	sow	sow	
	Sweet rocket (Hesperis matronalis)					
	Sweet William (Dianthus barbatus)					
	Wallflower (Erysimum cheiri)					
	Wild carrot (Daucus carota)		sow	sow	sow	
	Zinnia				sow	sow

Early summer	Midsummer	Late summer	Early autumn	Mid-autumn	Late autumn	Early winter
plant	plant			plant		
			plant	plant	plant	
plant out						
			plant	plant	plant	
				plant		
					plant	plant
			sow			
			sow			
		sow				
			sow			
sow	sow		plant out			
sow	sow		plant out			
			sow			
			sow			
			sow			
sow	sow		plant out			
				sow	sow	
sow	sow		plant out			
sow	sow		plant out			
sow	sow		plant out			

Notes

✿ Hardy and half-hardy annuals sown in spring will take 12–14 weeks to flower.

✿ Sowing outdoors in early or mid-spring should be done only if the soil has started to warm up.

✿ Early sowings will benefit from protection in the form of fleece or cloches.

✿ Half-hardy annuals are best started off indoors. Sow them 6–8 weeks before your probable last frost date. Adjust your timings according to your local conditions.

✿ Plant up dahlia tubers into large pots in early spring and keep protected from frost. They are tender so plant out on to your cut flower patch only when all danger of frost has passed.

Cutting patch
calendar

Midwinter	Make plans
	Order seeds
	Clean tools
Late winter	Buy in plant foods such as comfrey or seaweed fertiliser
	Order plug plants
	Sow sweet peas
	Sow some half-hardy annuals
Early spring	Weed plot and spread compost
	Rake in seaweed meal on to the cutting patch
	Pot up dahlia tubers indoors and protect from frost
	Plant out autumn-sown sweet peas
	Sow hardy annuals indoors
	Watch out for slugs
Mid-spring	Plant out hardy annuals
	Sow half-hardy annuals indoors
	Put in plant supports
	Weed the cut flower patch
	Water when needed
	Pinch out growing tips
	Visit local coppice supplier and collect hazel poles and pea sticks
	Direct sow hardy annuals
	Prick out and pot on seedlings
	Pot on plug plants when they arrive
	Buy comfrey plants
Late spring	Plant out half-hardy annuals once danger of frost has passed
	Weed the cut flower patch
	Water when needed
	Pinch out growing tips
	Lift daffodils bulbs, dry and store
	Tie in plants to supports as they grow

Early summer	Weed the cut flower patch
	Water when needed
	Deadhead flowers regularly
	Plant out half-hardy annuals and tender plants
	Sow biennials
	Lift daffodil and tulip bulbs, dry and store or replant elsewhere
	Tie in plants to their supports as they grow
Midsummer	Weed the cut flower patch
	Water when needed
	Deadhead flowers regularly
	Sow biennials
	Feed dahlias every week
Late summer	Weed the cut flower patch
	Water when needed
	Deadhead flowers regularly
	Feed dahlias every week
Early autumn	Water when needed
	Deadhead flowers regularly
	Sow hardy annuals for overwintering
	Plant daffodil bulbs
Mid-autumn	Plant bulbs
	Mulch cutting patch with compost
Late autumn	Plant tulips
	Lift dahlias when blackened by first frost
	Sow sweet peas
Early winter	Put your feet up and study seed catalogues

Favoured
resources

Where I can, I like to use small local companies. There are some excellent businesses out there that can help make your cutting patch a reality in a sustainable way. Here are some of my favourites.

Seeds

Benjamin Raynard at The Higgledy Garden specialises in selling cut flower seeds. He has a great website packed full of information and great photos to inspire. www.higgledygarden.com

Sarah Raven sells an extensive range of flower seeds. Her seed catalogues are stunning, with sumptuous photographs and excellent information. www.sarahraven.com

The Organic Gardening Catalogue might be better known for its vegetable seeds but it also has a good selection of flower seeds and indicates which are great for cutting. www.organiccatalog.com

Derry Watkins is a passionate plantswoman and has a great variety of annual and perennial seeds available from her online seed shop. If you can make it to her nursery just outside Bath, UK, there are plants to purchase too. www.specialplants.net

Kings Seeds offer a great selection of sweet peas and sell the pure white sweet William. www.kingsseeds.com

Roger Parsons is a specialist seed supplier of sweet peas with good information on those with the strongest scent and those that are good for cutting. www.rpsweetpeas.co.uk

Bulbs

Peter Nyssen is a bulb specialist. Good-quality bulbs and competitive prices mean growing them as cut flowers does not have to be costly. The company also sells a range of 'Karma' dahlias and has a good selection of herbaceous perennials. www.peternyssen.com

R.A. Scamp specialises in daffodil bulbs, with many of them grown in Cornwall, UK. www.qualitydaffodils.co.uk

Sarah Raven sells bulbs too. The prices are not as economical, but if you want some unusual cut flowers from bulbs this is the place to go. www.sarahraven.com

Plants

Primulas – For the smaller, more delicate primulas, rather than the big bedding varieties on sale at garden centres, it is advisable to look for a specialist nursery. I like Barnhaven Primroses (www.barnhaven.com) and Cath's Garden Plants (www.cathsgardenplants.co.uk) which are both mail order. Bodmin Plant & Herb Nursery (www.bodminnursery.co.uk) in Cornwall, UK, has a good selection if you live in the area, or are passing by.

Thompson and Morgan (www.thompson-morgan.com) sell a range of cut flowers as plug plants, as does Sarah Raven.

To find **independent plant nurseries** use the online British Plant Nursery Guide. The site also sells biodegradable pots made from corn starch.
www.britishplantnurseryguide.co.uk

For advice on **potentially harmful plants** visit http://apps.rhs.org.uk/advicesearch/Profile.aspx?pid=524. For **cats**, go to www.fabcats.org/owners/poisons/plants.html. For **dogs**, visit www.dogstrust.org.uk/az/factsheetsanddownloads/factsheetpoisonoussubstances09.pdf/

Equipment

The Organic Gardening Catalogue is an excellent place for everything garden related. Eco-containers, seaweed feeds, comfrey pellets, you name it, they stock it. This is the place to get your 'Bocking 14' comfrey plants.
www.organiccatalog.com

Hen and Hammock is a company that sources sustainably made products including wooden seed trays, wooden plant labels and a vase made out of recycled cardboard.
www.henandhammock.co.uk

Burgon and Ball offer a good selection of garden tools.
www.burgonandball.com

Haws sell a wide range of watering cans.
www.haws.co.uk

Nutscene produce natural jute twine. They have lots of other garden products too.
www.nutscene.com

For copper balls to clean your vases, try the homeware shop **Lakeland**.
www.lakeland.co.uk

Coppice products – To find somewhere to buy coppiced posts, bean poles and twiggy pea sticks there is an excellent website where you can search for your nearest supplier.
www.coppice-products.co.uk

Vases

Look out for recycled glass vases. **Nkuku** has a good range. www.nkuku.com

Markets and vintage fairs take place across the country throughout the year. The International Antiques & Collectors Fairs website is a good place to start a search.
www.iacf.co.uk

There are growing numbers of companies that will do the hard work for you, finding pieces at house clearances, auctions and markets and then selling them on. Google for them.

Mabel and Rose is a vintage shop based in Oxfordshire, UK. They sell an eclectic mix of finds picked up from their trips to markets overseas. With beautiful vases and unusual containers they offer quirky ways to display your flowers.
www.mabelandrose.com

Why not take a look at **Oxfam**'s online vintage shop. Browse through the pages of glassware and china from the comfort of your own home.
www.oxfam.org.uk/shop/vintage

For something that little bit different and special why not search for a glassmaker or ceramicist? I came across **Tara Davidson** and her beautiful vases (see image on page 157) while visiting Gloucestershire, UK/
www.tarajaneceramics.co.uk

The Crafts Council have an excellent website where you can search for a whole variety of craftspeople.
www.craftscouncil.org.uk

Index

numbers in *italics* refer to captions

LEFT Keep your flower
arrangements simple
by using only a few
stems of flowers such
as chrysanthemums,
and enjoy the fruits of
your labour.

Acknowledgments

Firstly, an enormous 'Thank you' to everyone at Frances Lincoln who worked on this book: to Andrew Dunn for saying 'yes'; to Becky Clarke for her beautiful design; and to Helen Griffin for her ambition for this book. A huge thanks to my editor, Joanna Chisholm, for her attention to detail and for pulling everything together.

I still can't quite believe my good fortune in having had the opportunity to work with such a hugely talented photographer as Jason Ingram. His skill, creativity and patience meant that it has been a real pleasure to work together, and the book really wouldn't have been the same without his stunning images.

Much love to my mum and dad for sowing the seeds of a lifelong love of all things botanical.

A huge thank you to the following:

Robin and Netty at www.vintagecratesuk.co.uk; Vanessa Arbuthnott (www.vanessaarbuthnott.co.uk) for her stunning fabric; Phil Hopkinson at www.malverncoppicing.co.uk; Andrew at Hen & Hammock for the amazing cardboard vase and your kind words; and to Philip Norman at the Garden Museum.

I have been immensely touched by the kindness of those who have helped in some way during the process.

To Bill Howe for coming to the rescue.

To Lynne Lawson of Barnhaven Primroses for your advice and for introducing me to Roy Genders's book on primulas.

To Karen Lynes at Peter Nyssen for all your help and advice when it felt like the weather was conspiring against me. You were so generous with your time.

To Sara Willman, you're a star. Thank you for sharing the bounty of your seed-sowing exploits. Your kindness and generosity have meant a great deal, and your mum makes mighty fine scones. And if it hadn't been for this book we may never have met.

Thank you Clover for the primrose picking. Yours were the stars of the show.

To Trevor, my fellow allotment holder – your own flower growing is an inspiration.

To my friends in the worlds of blogging, Twitter and Instagram, who have provided welcome relief during the long hours of writing. You are an amazing group of people, full of inspiration, advice and humour.

And finally to my husband, Ian. It was your idea at the very beginning that made me think maybe I could do it. Thank you for accompanying me on yet another quest for the perfect vase and turning your hand to pretty much everything, whether it was tracking down props, building a greenhouse, salvaging lost text from the black hole of the computer's memory or proofreading. In so many ways this has been a joint effort. But most of all, thank you for your never-ending support, patience and encouragement. I really couldn't have produced this book without you.